C

THE SOCIAL ANXIETY COGNITIVE BEHAVIORAL THERAPY WORKBOOK FOR ADULTS

A Cognitive Behavioral Therapy and Positive Psychology Guide to Overcome Anxiety, Fear, Worry, And Panic—Calm Your Thoughts With Mindfulness

MARCEE A. MARTIN

Improve Your Mental Health, Cure Your Social Anxiety, and Calm Your Thoughts

Social anxiety is not the same as shyness. Someone with social anxiety who may experience impaired functioning in certain social contexts may be extroverted and outgoing in other contexts. The general understanding of what social anxiety entails is quite low in society, and this may be why less than 25% of people with social anxiety receive adequate treatment (South African Depression and Anxiety Group, 2004). It's hard to treat a problem that you don't understand. Worse still, it's impossible to begin addressing an issue if you can't recognize that you have a problem to begin with. If you're unsure of whether or not you're dealing with social anxiety, try to reflect and notice if any of these issues apply to you. You often feel anxious when you think about or are engaged in a social situation, and this anxiety drains your energy and prevents you from living your life to the fullest. Your constant and uncontrollable states of anxiety, depression, and panic have taken over your life and are hindering your productivity. You've tried to overcome your anxiety, fear, worry, and panic on your own, but you've never been able to. You want to learn how to overcome your anxiety in a simple, practical, and modern way so you can unlock your highest potential, achieve your deepest desires, and delve into the world of productivity. If these pains and problems apply to you, then you may be dealing with social anxiety. If that's the case, then you need a valuable resource on overcoming anxiety that explains how to identify its triggers and the skills to prevent anxious thoughts, especially in social settings. You need a guide on cognitive behavioral therapy (CBT) techniques and other tested tools and strategies like mindfulness that will help you overcome anxiety, panic, worry, fear, and depression and take back control of your life. In essence, you need a CBT workbook that contains worksheets and guided exercises that will help you overcome social anxiety, fear, worry, and panic, and achieve a calmer state of mind.

In other words, you need this book. As a social anxiety CBT workbook for adults, this book can address all the pain and problems you suffer from your condition. Whether it's the emotional distress you experience or the impaired social functioning that plagues you, this book is a detailed guide that will provide you with step-by-step instructions on how to create and maintain your own mental health. That's not the only benefit you stand to gain. This book is also a comprehensive guide on social anxiety, how to identify its triggers, the necessary skills to prevent anxious thoughts, things to do, and things not to do to overcome social anxiety for good. This book even offers CBT techniques, positive psychology exercises, as well as other tools and strategies like mindfulness that focus on helping you reclaim control over your life and overcome anxiety, depression, fear, worry, panic, and any other distressing emotions. You will be guided carefully through exercises, activities, and worksheets focused on slaying your psychological demons associated with social anxiety. There are various lessons and advice that you will receive as you continue reading. To name a few, you will learn about what social anxiety really is, the root causes of social anxiety, the roles of worry, panic, and fear in social anxiety, the principles of CBT and how they work in treating social anxiety, how to understand the cognitive approach to dealing with social anxiety, how to challenge cognitive distortions and negative thoughts plaguing you, how to challenge the behaviors that have become habits that cause social anxiety, mindfulness meditation in calming anxiety issues, CBT-based exercises, positive psychology exercises, daily activities that can help you build an anxiety-free life, and a whole lot more!

To enable you to effectively receive all these benefits and lessons, this social anxiety workbook is divided into three parts for easy assimilation. The first part focuses on helping you understand exactly what you're up against when it comes to your social anxiety issues. The second part takes you through a simplified but highly effective step-by-step cognitive behavioral therapy approach to help you face your anxiety issues head-on and find lasting solutions. The third and final part of the book strongly helps in cheering you on in your battle against social anxiety and giving you further tips and advice on how to stay permanently anxiety free as you live your day-to-day life. Part 1: You Gotta Understand What You're Up Against consists of Chapters 1, 2, and 3. Chapter 1: The Anxiety Whiplash focuses on explaining exactly what social anxiety looks and feels like. You will explore the emotions and behaviors linked to social anxiety. Chapter 2: Accompanying Demons will focus on what exactly causes social anxiety and what else can aggravate it. This will help you understand social anxiety more and how to prevent it. Chapter 3: Deep Dive: Worry and Panic will zoom in on the roles of worry and panic in social anxiety. There are several emotions involved in social anxiety, but worry and panic are the more important, prevalent, and significant emotions.

Part 2: Cognitive Behavioral Therapy: A Real, Helpful, and Simply Approach contains Chapters 4, 5, and 6. Chapter 4: Understand Why CBT Is Worth It will teach you the principles behind CBT and why they effectively address social anxiety. This can help you gain confidence in the CBT methods you will learn. Chapter 5: Challenging Cognitive Distortions About Your Anxiety will lead you to cooperate with your thoughts. Often with social anxiety, your thoughts can work against you and be your worst enemies. This chapter will teach you how to make your thoughts your support. Chapter 6: Behavioral Therapy to Take Back Control of

Your Life focuses on challenging the behaviors that have become habits over time and now exacerbate your social anxiety. Part 3: Crush Anxiety, Go, Go, Go! is made up of Chapters 7 and 8. Chapter 7: Mindfulness Exercises and Coping Skills will guide you through mindfulness meditation exercises and other techniques that are useful in calming your mind and decreasing your anxiety. Chapter 8: CBT-Based Exercises, Positive Psychology Exercises, and Daily Activities to Maintain an Anxiety-Free Life will end this book by providing you with helpful exercises and activities. These final exercises will focus on preventing relapses, making your daily life free of social anxiety, and helping you enjoy your life free from panic and worry.

I have confidence in the contents of this book as all these knowledge, exercises, and worksheets are what helped me in my own battle with social anxiety. As I was struggling to conquer my social anxiety on my own, I made a lot of mistakes. But those mistakes shaped my expertise in this field, so now I'm sharing what I know so that you don't have to make the same mistakes I did. Currently, I like to call myself the happiest author on planet earth, but my journey to inner happiness was long, protracted, often complex, but fulfilling in the end. This journey began when I was in my late twenties when I finally got tired of the emotional whirlpool I had been stuck in since my early teen years and made the decision to change my life. Up until then, I had suffered from low self-esteem, chronic anxiety, non-existent self-confidence, and a plethora of other emotional disorders.

Of all these issues, social anxiety was the most obvious to me at times since this issue affected my relationships with others. But being uninformed about this disorder and indifferent toward my mental health as a teenager, my social anxiety was left to run rampant. It got to a point where I was only ever calm within the safety and peace of my room. And sometimes, the anxiety could even find me there. Essentially, there was nowhere that was safe—nowhere that I could go to be free of my self-doubt, low energy, negative thoughts, and feelings of inadequacy. As I got older, my social anxiety started to affect my romantic relationships too. They all seemed to end in the same manner—in a cloud of emotional imbalance, suspicion, toxicity, and unmatched energy. Even my professional life was damaged. I dreaded social gatherings and networking events. Every party or office meeting brought out the worst of my inner demons, and I would often make up excuses to miss them, which didn't endear me to my colleagues or my bosses. There is a very social aspect to the workplace, but my social anxiety didn't allow me to participate. Moreover, though I had the aptitude and skills that would help me flourish at my job, this didn't become a reality as I was too afraid to voice out any of my ideas. I hated the sound of my own voice in the presence of other people, and I felt like I always managed to say the wrong things. These emotions led me to always beat myself up if I spoke up in social situations. Social anxiety was eating away at every aspect of my life, and I was thoroughly miserable.

Then, on the brink of a total mental and emotional breakdown, I decided that I wanted to make a change. I started a quest in search of true happiness and emotional balance. I read over 100 books across several niches and watched over 200 informative videos. Eventually, the secrets of human relationships and psychology that I unearthed during this period of intense research transformed my life. The principles I found helped me to rebuild my relationship with myself, learn self-love, and improve my communication skills with other people. Now, for the last five years, my new quest has been bringing others closer to happiness by writing about my experiences and the knowledge I've gained. The pillars of my teachings revolve around mindfulness and meditation techniques for anxiety, depression, and stress, the importance of listening (and not just hearing), ways to challenge and fix cognitive distortions, the best ways to communicate even during difficult times, new methods to shape and discuss with your inner critic, CBT techniques for restoring emotional balance, the importance of self-love, self-esteem, and self-confidence, how to deepen empathetic traits without becoming codependent, coaching to build conversational skills, learning to develop charisma and using witty banter to great effect, and body language clues and how to read between the lines (I believe that everyone can communicate better if they know how to listen to others and read their body language). I was born shy, but I have come to realize that with the right approach, anybody can become a great conversationalist and people's magnet. My life mission is to teach this approach to others and to lead them to be more confident, assured people with better mental health.

I have written this book with this intention in mind and because I am passionate about helping people overcome issues with their social anxiety, such as serious fear and panic in social settings. I believe that I can offer significant aid to those suffering from social anxiety as I've been studying the best methods for overcoming social anxiety for at least five years now. Helping you achieve freedom from the constant plague of social anxiety and panic matters deeply to me because all of what you're about to learn are tools and tricks that helped me overcome my own struggles with these issues. Through the contents of this book, I became better at holding my own out there without letting extreme nervousness snatch great experiences from my hands. I strongly believe that this book can do the same for you. I understand how difficult and daunting it might seem to want to start pulling apart the topic of social anxiety, and, as such, I can show you how to work things out without stress. I'm confident that the strategies I share with you here will help you immensely as I've had practical experience with these issues in the past. I promise you that this book can help you understand the basics and must-knows of social anxiety that are practical and applicable to you. After you read this book, you will be able to start getting rid of anxiety, anger, and worry for good. Aside from the importance of addressing your social anxiety, it's also vital to understand mental health at this time to avoid cluelessness or ignorance. So the sooner you start learning, the sooner you will be more informed about yourself and your condition. This way, the next time you come face to face with intense anxiety, you'll know exactly what to do. So without further ado, let's dive right into the book. The first chapter will explore social anxiety itself so that you understand this condition more.

Chapter One
THE ANXIETY WHIPLASH

This chapter aims to help you understand exactly what social anxiety is about. To achieve this, you will explore what social anxiety is not (such as everyday nervousness and shyness) and what constitutes social anxiety (that is, its signs, symptoms, descriptions, causes, and dangers). These are all important and foundational details you will need on your healing journey.

WHAT ANXIETY IS NOT

Before you start learning all about social anxiety, let's take a step back first and clearly define what anxiety is not. This way, you won't get confused later on as you learn more about anxiety. It can be easy to mistake anxiety for something else or to mislabel certain emotions as anxiety. So now, let's differentiate between anxiety and the two common emotions that are often conflated with it. These two emotions are everyday nervousness and shyness.

Every person experiences nervousness now and then. But it can be hard to determine whether you're feeling nervous or anxious if you don't understand both concepts well enough. The main difference is that nervousness is a common emotion that everyone faces in their day-to-day lives, while anxiety is a diagnosable medical condition. Nervousness can be defined as feeling excited, worried, or even a bit afraid, and there is usually a specific trigger that you're feeling nervous about. On the other hand, anxiety is more extreme fear and worry about a wide range of potential issues. Another difference is that nervousness is a short-term emotion. Once the trigger situation is over, your nervousness fades away. But anxiety is a long-term condition. Even after your current source of anxiety is dealt with, you may continue worrying about it after the fact. Or you will start feeling anxious about the next situation. Anxiety doesn't stop once its source is dealt with. Instead, it applies itself to other parts of your life. If you're nervous, you will later be able to feel relief from your nervousness. If you have anxiety, you will feel anxious almost every day and struggle to recall the last time you felt totally relaxed. Nervousness can be useful to you as it's often a response to something specific. In this way, your nervousness serves a function of alerting you to things that may be dangerous or threatening. It's not a nice feeling, but you should listen to it as it's fundamentally trying to help you. And once you deal with the situation, making it less dangerous or threatening, your nervousness will fade. This suggests how your nervousness only aims to keep you safe. Meanwhile, your anxiety is an illness that constantly comes in waves without needing a specific event to trigger it. You will simply feel constantly anxious. And even when your anxiety is focusing on a specific event, chances are that it's not a realistic or rational worry. Thus, your anxiety doesn't serve any purpose and only functions to give you undue emotional distress.

One of the biggest differences between simple nervousness and anxiety is that anxiety can lead to dark thoughts. Since nervousness is focused on a specific event that you can change to reduce your nervousness, you will be more concentrated on the positive actions that you can take to improve your situation and solve your nervousness. However, anxiety isn't always focused on a single event, and even when it is, it's not always a situation that you can change or improve. This vague distress over something you have no control over will suspend you in inaction, and you will inevitably begin to focus on your thoughts rather than your actions. And the discomfort and unpleasantness of anxiety can be so unbearable that your thoughts are led to some very dark and difficult places. This can then lead to maladaptive behaviors, such as self-harm or other self-damaging acts (like smoking, drinking, or gambling) in an attempt to cope with your anxiety. In the most extreme cases of anxiety, your dark thoughts can even lead to thoughts of suicide as your anxiety becomes so unbearable that you think suicide is the only way to escape from it. The dark thoughts caused by your anxiety can be persistent and all-consuming. Another difference between nervousness and anxiety is that anxiety can interfere with your life. Since nervousness is short-term, you can easily deal with it and continue on with your life. You may feel nervous about doing certain things, but you're usually able to do those things anyway despite the nervousness you feel. But with anxiety, your emotions may be so intense that you're hindered from doing the things you're anxious about. This can significantly interfere with your day-to-day life. You may begin to avoid the things that make you anxious, let go of opportunities because of your fears, or damage certain relationships due to your anxiety. All this can be very limiting and harmful to your life. There will be many things that you will miss out on or feel like you can't due simply because of how anxiety causes you to feel.

Next, social anxiety is not the same as shyness, though it is often dismissed as such. This may be why people with social anxiety often don't seek help —because they don't know they're dealing with a recognized psychiatric condition. To help you distinguish between the two, let's explore what exactly shyness entails. Shyness can be understood as a feeling of discomfort or nervousness, usually in response to your fear of social situations. Shyness is often linked with low self-esteem, excessive self-consciousness, negative self-evaluations, and negative self-preoccupations. Shyness can be characterized by you being reserved and timid in new situations, when among strangers, or even when approaching or being approached by someone you know. The common signs of shyness are that you have negative feelings about yourself, you worry about how others may view you, often you want to withdraw or avoid social interactions altogether, blushing, sweating, increased heart rates, or stomach issues. There are a few possible causes of shyness. The first is a poor sense of self. All the signs and symptoms of shyness you've read above have all had to do with a sense of self. That is, your self-perception, self-esteem, self-consciousness, self-evaluations, and self-preoccupations. If you had a healthy sense of self, you would have good self-perception and self-esteem, you wouldn't be too self-conscious or self-preoccupied, and you would have realistic self-evaluations. This all combines to form a balanced and confident individual. However, if you have a poor sense of self, all these traits will be damaged and unhealthy. Thus, you may become unconfident, unassertive, and shy. A sense of self is developed from childhood and is affected by various factors, such as your upbringing, your environment, and genetics. This is to say that you're not born with shyness. Rather, shyness is developed within you just like any other trait. Other causes for shyness include biological and environmental factors. Social experiences can affect your levels of shyness, especially your social interactions with your parents. Overprotective parents can inadvertently raise their children to be shy, unconfident, and have difficulty developing social skills. Perhaps such parents never gave their children the chance to venture out, make their own mistakes, and stand on their own. Thus the children never get the chance to become confident in themselves. This can lead to a weak sense of self and high levels of shyness.

Now compare the description above to this. Social anxiety is a major type of anxiety disorder that includes fear or apprehension about social interactions and performance situations. Someone with social anxiety may feel afraid or worried about public speaking, engaging in meetings or classes, meeting new people, going to social events or activities, picking up a random phone call, or expressing their opinions to others. The main theme of worry for social anxiety is exposure to judgment, criticism, scrutiny, or rejection in a social or performance situation. The common signs and symptoms of social anxiety are feelings of humiliation or embarrassment, fear about interacting with strangers, overanalyzing your performance, being overly critical about your performance, avoiding circumstances where you may end up being the center of attention, blushing, increased heart rates, trembling, feeling lightheaded, or stomach issues. However, this is just a condensed, simplified list of symptoms. A more extensive list will be provided in the next section. In the same way, here is a simplified list of potential causes for social anxiety. Much like shyness, social anxiety isn't something that you're born with but rather something that develops within you as a result of a bunch of interlinking factors. Genetics plays a role, as do environmental factors such as your social interactions during your developmental years. For example, if you were raised in a controlling or overprotective environment, you may be more at risk of developing social anxiety. The same could be said for if you experienced abuse, bullying, divorce of your parents, or family conflict as you were growing up. These negative experiences can lead you to become socially anxious.

If you compare these two descriptions of shyness and of social anxiety, you can see that they share many characteristics. This is undeniable. But you can understand the fundamental differences between shyness and social anxiety if you view them as points on a spectrum. In that case, shyness can be seen as a much milder version of social anxiety. So their symptoms may be very similar, but the intensity at which you experience them are vastly different, and thus the resultant behaviors expressed can be very different. So shy people may feel fear and anxiety to some degree, but these emotions will usually not result in many maladaptive behaviors and habits. People with social anxiety will feel fear and anxiety to a high degree, and these emotions will almost always lead them to adopt several maladaptive strategies and behaviors. So the main differences between shyness and social anxiety are the intensity of distress, impairment of functioning, and level of avoidance. People with shyness experience lower levels of distress that don't pose a threat or impediment to their normal functioning. This means that they aren't led to avoid any particular situation. People with social anxiety experience high levels of distress that impede and hinder their normal functioning and disrupt their daily lives. This leads to avoidant behaviors where social situations are seen as scary and overwhelming. Someone with social anxiety won't just feel nervous before giving a speech (which is about the extent of the symptoms experienced by someone with shyness). Someone with social anxiety may worry about the speech for days or weeks in advance. Their anxiety may affect their physical body, leading to loss of sleep, racing heartbeats, shortness of breath, sweating or shaking. And these symptoms may not go away but worsen as the situation nears. In this scenario, even if the individual recognizes that their fears are unfounded or that they have no control over the situation, their anxiety may not leave, and they will continue to suffer. So though most people with social anxiety experience symptoms of shyness, those who are shy don't always experience social anxiety.

UNDERSTANDING SOCIAL ANXIETY, ITS SIGNS, AND ITS DANGERS

Now that you know what social anxiety is not, let's define what it is. Social anxiety is a long-term, overwhelming fear of social situations. This fear is irrational and constant, and it can affect your everyday activities, normal functioning, self-confidence, relationships, work life, and school life. Though it's a normal phenomenon to worry about social situations occasionally, social anxiety causes you to worry before, during, and after them. Anxiety is a normal response to stress, so it's not inherently a negative emotion. The problem arises when the anxiety doesn't go away even after the stressor is over. This is the case for anxiety disorders. Removing the cause of the stress doesn't help to reduce the emotion itself. This is the distinction between anxiety and being anxious. Being anxious is simply a reaction to stress, and this doesn't usually significantly impair your life or cause you undue emotional distress. Anxiety is when the emotion begins disrupting your quality of life. A good way to think about it to help you distinguish between anxiety and being anxious is to consider them as a spectrum. Being anxious falls on the moderate part of this spectrum, where it can help you better prepare for things to come or alert you to any dangerous situations. This is a normal reaction to stress. Anxiety falls on the extreme part of this spectrum, where your reaction is out of proportion to the situation and actually impairs your ability to function normally. So while being anxious can help you in a situation, anxiety obstructs you from performing in a situation. When it gets to this stage, you should be aware of your anxiety levels and begin seeking help. Another way to know that you should seek help for your anxiety is that you will exhibit abnormal and excessive anticipatory responses when faced with uncertainty. This means that you may anticipate the uncertainty and possible outcomes in a way that's not realistic or proportionate to the actual situation. Further, you will have exaggerated and constant worries that won't go away, despite there being any reason for you to feel anxious. If all these descriptions relate to you, and if you think your anxiety is interfering with your everyday life and worsening your quality of life, then you must make the decision to begin addressing this issue.

Now that you understand the definition of social anxiety, let's explore an extensive list of its symptoms so that you are more aware of the signs of social anxiety. There are three main categories of symptoms: physical, emotional, and behavioral. These are the three ways in which social anxiety will express itself in an individual. These symptoms are distinctive and unique and quite difficult to be ignored or written off by the one suffering from them. Others may also notice that something is off with social anxiety sufferers, but they usually won't understand the intensity and severity of the anxiety being experienced. If you suffer from social anxiety, then social encounters may often produce a strong and instant physical response in you which can be extremely distressing and hard to control. This makes the overall experience of the symptoms highly unpleasant. Some physical symptoms caused by severe social anxiety are (Mayo Clinic, 2017):

- elevated heart rate
- sweating of the palms
- blushing
- shakiness or trembling
- chest tightness or a choking sensation
- dry mouth
- dizziness or fear of fainting
- awkward and stumbling speech
- muscle pain and tension, usually in the upper body
- slowed thinking processes or an inability to focus or concentrate

These physical symptoms are similar to the symptoms experienced during a panic attack (though social anxiety and panic attacks are two completely separate issues) or when you're involved in an accident or situation where you feel threatened with bodily harm. It's notable that these reactions, despite sharing similarities with reactions produced when you're being realistically threatened with harm, occur during social encounters that realistically pose no physical threat to you. These social encounters that produce such harrowing physical symptoms in you would be considered benign or harmless by most. Severe social anxiety responses are intense, overwhelming, and disproportionate to any potential threat.

Another intense category of symptoms is the psychological and emotional symptoms of social anxiety. These symptoms can be significant and disabling. Though they only occur in your mind, the harm caused can be dire. If you have social anxiety, the emotions produced during interactions with other people can crush you as you will be excessively self-conscious, reflect only on worst-case scenarios, experience extremely low self-esteem, and beat yourself up for any mistakes you made. The psychological and emotional symptoms that are caused by this include:

- intense fear of being negatively judged, typically based on inadequate social performance
- constant worry about saying or doing something embarrassing
- feelings of severe awkwardness or inferiority around authority figures
- a fear that others will notice the social

anxiety sufferer's discomfort and reject them because of it

- extreme reluctance to express opinions or initiate conversations, caused by a fear of being dismissed as stupid, incompetent, or pushy
- a disproportionate (and uncomfortable) feeling of giddiness or satisfaction at being praised or applauded by others
- a powerful desire to never be the center of attention
- anticipatory anxiety (a debilitating fear of social situations before they arise)
- feelings of shame and inferiority during actual social encounters
- harsh self-judgments following conversations or other interactions with people

These symptoms all center around fears and these fears are almost never based on a realistic assessment of probable outcomes. Nonetheless, the force of these fears can be overwhelming, making you desperate to avoid any situations that would trigger your social anxiety and lead to these symptoms.

Finally, you have the behavioral symptoms of social anxiety. The emotional and physical symptoms mentioned before can lead you to develop avoidant habits where you simply avoid situations that you find highly stressful or potentially threatening. These habits can be extremely limiting and harmful. If you begin to avoid certain social situations, then several parts of your life will be affected, such as forming new friendships, engaging in romantic relationships, applying for jobs, pursuing your interests, attending college, taking lessons from others, getting involved in sports, or volunteering to help in causes that you support. Regardless of your other emotions (passion, interest, curiosity, connection), you may choose to forgo certain experiences to avoid triggering your social anxiety. Such behavior may sabotage your happiness and satisfaction in life. The types of social situations that you may avoid are:

- parties or intimate gatherings with people you don't know well
- interactions with authority figures or well-known, accomplished individuals
- being introduced to new people in settings where conversation is expected

- taking or making phone calls
- asking for assistance in stores, in restaurants, from public servants, or from people on the street
- job- or school-related interviews
- performing in front of an audience (such as playing a sport or musical instrument, public speaking, and so on)
- family reunions where more distant relatives are present
- encounters with people you knew in the past (such as old schoolmates, co-workers, and so on) who you think might judge you for your lack of life progress
- standing in line at stores, banks, or government offices with people who want to chat
- dating or any situation that offers the possibility of more intimate interpersonal interactions
- internet chat rooms or forums where negative feedback or personal criticism can be expected

Next, let's explore the possible explanations for why you have social anxiety. One major component is genetics. If you have any first-degree relatives with an anxiety disorder or with environmental concerns that make them more at risk of anxiety disorders (such as child abuse or substance abuse), then they may have passed certain genes down to you—genes that make you more vulnerable to developing an anxiety disorder. Your brain structure is also a factor. Different parts of your brain are responsible for different functions, so the size and functioning of your brain play a role in your susceptibility to anxiety disorders. In particular, the areas of your brain that control your fear responses and the storing and retrieval of your emotional and fear-related memories. Other than that, your personality traits (such as your shyness and nervousness in childhood), life history (such as being exposed to negative or stressful life events), other health conditions (for example, thyroid problems can make you more prone to anxiety), and use of certain stimulants (such as caffeine) can contribute to and worsen your symptoms of anxiety. Another way to understand your anxiety is that it is an instinctual response to danger that is functioning overtime. As humans evolved, we relied on our fear response, which is our fight or flight response. Our sympathetic nervous systems made our bodies react quickly when we were in danger to increase our chances of survival. Anxiety and fear evolved as an alarm bell to initiate that response. Currently, you no longer face life-threatening situations, but your nervous system continues to react with your fight or flight response, even when it isn't necessary. This is why you feel anxiety. So to overcome your anxiety, you simply need to teach your body and mind how to redirect your energies. But more on how to overcome anxiety later.

Now, let's move on to the last bit of information for this chapter, which is the dangers of leaving your anxiety unchecked. Firstly, leaving your anxiety unchecked can often lead to depression. These two disorders often occur together, and they have several overlapping symptoms. Both involve agitation, insomnia, difficulty concentrating, and anxiety. This can then lead to the issue of suicide. A high percentage of people who die by suicide have been diagnosed with some sort of mental illness. This includes anxiety and depression. So to ensure your physical and mental safety, you must take positive action to address your social anxiety. Another issue that can be caused by social anxiety is substance abuse. Having an anxiety disorder places you at a greater risk for addiction to several substances, such as alcohol, nicotine, and other drugs. You may begin abusing substances to relieve your symptoms or to help you feel happy. There's no evidence that alcohol relieves anxiety, but many people still believe that it can help them feel calmer and happier. And some people do report temporary relief from their anxiety while they're under the influence of certain substances. However, these are not long-term solutions. In fact, they will only lead to dependency, other issues (physical and mental), and may even exacerbate your anxiety. You may also develop various physical illnesses due to your social anxiety. Chronic stress (associated with anxiety) can severely compromise your immune system, thus making you more vulnerable to infections, colds, flu, and other viral and bacterial diseases.

Those are the short-term dangers of social anxiety. The long-term harms include the development of heart disease or the obstruction of recovery from heart disease. This is because your anxiety can interfere with several things that can stave off and heal the occurrence of heart diseases, such as regular exercise and a healthy diet. Your daily functioning and schedules will also be thrown askew as you will start living your life in accordance with your anxiety. If you feel too anxious to do this, you will procrastinate. If you feel too anxious to go here, you will avoid that place entirely. This will place several limits and confinements on your life. Finally, anxiety can result in brain damage and increase your risk of dementia later in life. Anxiety has been found to lead to structural degeneration in people's prefrontal cortex and hippocampus.

As a short exercise after learning all about social anxiety, try to go through the symptoms of social anxiety and list down the ones that apply to you. Ask yourself what happens to you when you get anxious. Write down all your answers so that you can later reflect on them. This will help you become more aware whenever you start feeling anxious. Noticing the problem is the first step in addressing it. Another short exercise you can do is to ask yourself what negative effects social anxiety has had on your life so far. Write down your answers. This can help you reflect on the quality of your life and solidify your determination and conviction to overcome your anxiety. In the next chapter, you will learn about the factors that can aggravate your social anxiety.

Chapter Two

ACCOMPANYING DEMONS

There is usually not any one specific reason that can be definitively said to have caused a certain mental illness. Typically, mental illnesses develop as a result of many contributing factors. So the root causes of social anxiety can't exactly be known in black and white, but there are several issues that can aggravate and contribute to the development of social anxiety disorder. These are what you may call the accompanying demons, which you will learn about in this chapter. There are seven main demons that may lead to social anxiety: childhood trauma, depression, abuse, low self-esteem, bullying, rejection or abandonment, and constant shaming (especially in public).

First off, childhood trauma is a big contributing factor to social anxiety later in life. Trauma can include abandonment, neglect, abuse (physical, sexual, or emotional), bullying, family conflicts (such as divorce or custody battles), domestic violence, the death of a loved one, postnatal depression or stress during pregnancy, and so on. Some of these traumas will be detailed later on (such as bullying and abandonment), but for now, you will focus on trauma as a general category and how it can lead to social anxiety. One way in which trauma can make you more inclined toward anxiety is in the way it affects your brain. Trauma can cause your amygdala to be more sensitive and active. Your amygdala is responsible for the activation of your fear response, that is, your fight or flight. This response leads to a wave of symptoms, such as increased heart rate, faster breathing, muscle tension, stomach issues, and a higher sense of stress. All these are symptoms of anxiety. So trauma can program your brain to create symptoms of anxiety more frequently, in response to stimuli that may not be realistically threatening. As your amygdala becomes more sensitive and hyperactive, you may begin to see threats in innocuous places. This description fits social anxiety perfectly, as people with social anxiety may perceive social interactions (which don't pose any real threat to their safety) as legitimate dangers, thus triggering their fight or flight response and the subsequent symptoms of anxiety. Another way trauma can lead to social anxiety is that it can contribute to the development of post-traumatic stress disorder (PTSD), which is another type of anxiety disorder. PTSD can link to social anxiety as people with PTSD may feel stigmatized due to their illness and thus avoid social situations. They may also experience immense shame and guilt (a symptom of PTSD) and thus socially isolate themselves. PTSD may even lead to depression, another socially crippling mental disorder that can make it difficult for them to maintain a healthy social life. Aside from these reasons, PTSD in itself can cause you a lot of anxiety. PTSD occurs when your nervous system doesn't fully recover or reset after a trauma. This can lead to four major symptoms: intrusion, where you have involuntary flashbacks, memories, and dreams about the past trauma; avoidance, where you try hard not to think or talk about the trauma, and you avoid places, people, and any other reminders; mood and cognition changes, where you experience distorted thoughts, such as blaming yourself for the trauma; and reactivity changes, where your behavior becomes irritable and reckless. All these symptoms can cause you endless amounts of anxiety, and in some cases, lead to social anxiety. When you're living with PTSD, you may experience a lot of social stress since certain social situations can trigger your PTSD. So you may become hypervigilant in social situations, making your social anxiety all the more provoking.

The next accompanying demon is depression. Social anxiety and depression can affect each other: If you have depression, you may eventually develop social anxiety, and if you have social anxiety, you may eventually develop depression. Depression can cause you to have low self-esteem, low self-confidence, high self-hate, high self-doubt, and erroneous beliefs that others don't like you. This can make social situations harrowing for you, and eventually, you may begin to avoid social settings as they make you nervous. If such behavior continues, you may subsequently develop social anxiety. On the other hand, if you have social anxiety, you may isolate yourself and hinder yourself from having any deep and meaningful relationships. You may indulge in erroneous and negative beliefs about yourself, and this may lead to depression. However, let's clarify one thing here. Though both depression and social anxiety involve the symptom of social withdrawal, the reason for this withdrawal differs between the two disorders. To illustrate, imagine a young university student who wants to make new friends and go to parties. However, she fears that she will embarrass herself in front of others and be laughed at. So she stays in her dorm room by herself every night, wishing she could pluck up the courage to go out and be with others. Now imagine a different scenario where this student avoids social settings and gatherings because it's simply not enjoyable for her. The thought of attending parties and being with others holds no allure or promise of pleasure. The first scenario represents someone with social anxiety who withdraws for fear of being negatively evaluated by others. The second scenario represents someone with depression who withdraws because they find no pleasure or happiness being with others. Someone with social anxiety thinks that they could enjoy themselves if they could only interact appropriately and successfully with others, while someone with depression doesn't think they can enjoy themselves at all. This is the main difference between social anxiety and depression, but over time, the reasons for social withdrawal can overlap. That being said, there are several other ways that depression and social anxiety overlap which makes it understandable how one condition can lead to the other. For example, both illnesses entail having anxiety when in an embarrassing situation with others, having anxiety when speaking in front of others, feelings of worthlessness, an inability to feel happy in certain circumstances, irritability, and unstable moods (especially when under stress).

Moving on, abuse (emotional, physical, mental, or sexual) is also a contributing factor to social anxiety. Abusive relationships often lead to anxiety. Maybe you experienced an abusive parent, an abusive partner, or domestic violence. And this abuse and violence isn't always physical. Many people brush off the abuse they experience simply because it's not obviously detrimental like physical abuse is. But emotional and mental abuse are equally as damaging. Perhaps more so because most people don't recognize it as abuse and thus don't try to protect themselves against it; emotional abuse can happen to anyone, male or female, young or old. Sometimes it can be blatant, but often it is subtle and normalized within a relationship. Sometimes, the abuser may not be aware that they are being emotionally abusive as no one ever educated them in this area. Other times, the abuser may be aware and may be consciously manipulating and abusing you. Either way, if you are being emotionally abused, then you are being hurt, controlled, manipulated, and threatened. For example, the abuser may threaten you if you do something they don't want you to do, frequently insult you and put you down with hurtful words, criticize you excessively and publicly, control your behaviors (including what you wear, what you do, where you can go, and who you can see), intimidate you (with threats of violence or threats of leaving), or manipulate you (such as gaslighting, constant lying, or emotional blackmail). Other, less noticeable forms of emotional abuse occur when the abuser gives you the silent treatment (where they refuse to talk to you as punishment for a random act you did), withholds affection in order to punish you or to get something from you, makes mean jokes that you're not okay with, goes through your phone, doesn't allow you any privacy, or blames you for anything that goes wrong. Nobody is perfect, so you may be guilty of doing one or two of these acts every once in a while. But someone who is emotionally abusive will do these acts daily with the intention of getting what they want from you or controlling you. When you're often emotionally abused, the abuser will have more power over how you think, feel, and act. And remember, abusive relationships aren't exclusive to romantic partners. It's possible that your friends or family members are emotionally abusive toward you as well. No matter who is emotionally abusing you, the adverse effects on you can be long-lasting and severe. You may feel like you can't do anything right (since you're often punished for random acts) or like you're worthless (since your self-esteem and confidence will be constantly undermined). You will feel sad, depressed, lonely, and afraid. This complete lack of peace may lead to anxiety. You may find it stressful to be around your abuser since anything you do can lead to punishment and humiliation. This anxiety can even leak out and affect other aspects of your life, such as your friendships and work. When you are constantly stressed within a relationship, you will develop certain habits that will continue that anxiety in other situations. These habits include overthinking, poor self-esteem, wondering when you will mess up again, and constantly being on edge. All these habits can trigger anxiety symptoms and eventually cause you to develop social anxiety.

Next, low self-esteem is a contributing factor to social anxiety. This has been stated previously in this chapter, but now you will explore this concept deeper. For starters, ask yourself what self-esteem is. This can help you understand how having low self-esteem can lead to having social anxiety. Self-esteem entails how you perceive and value yourself. If you have healthy self-esteem, you can view yourself realistically (all your strengths and weaknesses) and see yourself as a person of worth. But if you have low self-esteem, you will see yourself as worthless and unimportant. You will focus too heavily on your weaknesses and not enough on your strengths. You will be overly critical of yourself and often have negative thoughts and harsh judgments about yourself. There are a few reasons why your self-esteem may be low. Sometimes, low self-esteem is linked to an intense desire to be perfect—you feel pressured to be highly successful and constantly achieving. You may feel this pressure from others (like your friends, family, or teachers), society (or what you perceive as social standards and norms), or yourself (such as when you set impossibly high standards for yourself). Another factor of low self-esteem is a strong fear of failure, making mistakes, or looking stupid in front of others. Or your low self-esteem may have to do with your upbringing where your accomplishments weren't acknowledged, your mistakes were emphasized, you were constantly put down, or you were always negatively compared to others. Whatever the cause, having low self-esteem can impact how you function in the world as you may begin to find it difficult to be around others. When you have low self-esteem, you may always compare yourself to others and think that others are always better than you are. You will make these negative comparisons which create a cycle where you're constantly criticizing yourself, putting yourself down, looking for any flaws you may have, and not appreciating your strengths. All these habits will contribute to you feeling lousy about yourself, which will then intensify these habits. Overall, low self-esteem can make you feel like you're incomplete, lacking, or less than other people. You will only see your failures and others' successes and begin to hate yourself. Such emotions and thoughts can provoke your anxiety and potentially lead to social anxiety, where you dread being with other people, worry about making mistakes, have palpitations when in public, are overthinking, assuming the worst about yourself, and worrying excessively about social events. When you think about yourself negatively (as people with low self-esteem usually do), you become more prone to social anxiety as you will more easily believe that others don't like you, that you've embarrassed yourself, or that getting involved in a social situation will lead to your humiliation. But believing in these false thoughts will only lead you to avoid social events and thus decrease the chances that other people will react positively to you. When others don't have the chance to show you that they like you, it becomes even easier for you to believe that they're being critical about you or making fun of you. This creates a vicious cycle of low self-esteem and social anxiety where you withdraw further and further away from social connections.

Other than that, bullying is a negative experience that often contributes to the development of social anxiety. Bullying can relate to the previous category of trauma as being the target of bullying can be harrowing and cause your fight or flight response to become overactive. However, bullying isn't always traumatic, though it's definitely never easy or pleasant. Even if your experiences of bullying aren't coded as traumatic by your brain, the pain and distress you feel can still impact almost every aspect of your life, leaving you lonely, vulnerable, isolated, and anxious. These effects can continue even after the bully has been removed and you are in a safe environment. This is because you remember the stress caused by the instances of bullying, whether the bullying took on the form of physical violence, cyberbullying, or psychological violence. After being exposed to bullying for a long time, you may have developed adverse reactions and maladaptive habits. Some victims of bullying later experience eating disorders, depression, thoughts of suicide, and anxiety. To speak more on how bullying can lead to anxiety, you must understand that victims of bullying are often publicly ridiculed, humiliated, and assessed negatively by others. This can lead them to develop an intense fear of being criticized or embarrassed in front of others in the future. This fear can lead to social anxiety, where you're overly self-conscious and hypervigilant in normal social situations. This behavior stems from their memories of being bullied which led them to develop an apprehension that others will judge or ridicule them. They may worry about what they say, how they look, and what they do in an effort to avoid being negatively assessed by others.

On another tangent, fear of rejection can also

lead to social anxiety. In this context, rejection can mean being shunned or ignored by others in a social setting. This rejection can be intentional or accidental (the person you perceive as rejecting you may not even be aware of the effect of their actions). Either way, rejection is a common occurrence in life. Everyone has to experience it at some point, and the experience will usually not be pleasant. Being rejected hurts, and it can often etch a mark in your memory. Some examples of social rejection include being turned down after asking someone out on a date, being picked last in gym class, or not being invited to a social gathering. Humans are naturally social creatures, and so social rejection is seen as undesirable and painful. However, despite it being undesirable, some people still manage to handle rejection well. They can accept that rejection is a natural part of life and that some things are out of their control. They don't see social rejection as a negative comment on their overall worth as a person, and they can recognize that the rejection occurred in an isolated event and thus cannot be extended into general beliefs about their value or self. However, someone with social anxiety will not be able to realize any of this. They see rejection as a monstrous possibility.

This may be due to the fact that people with social anxiety deeply crave social interaction and acceptance from others, even though it causes them stress. This strong desire for socialization then leads them to demonize social rejection and react to it in extreme and exaggerated ways. When you don't achieve your desired socialization, you feel the pain of rejection which is simply your mind's way of telling you that a need has not been met. It's like being hungry. The feeling of hunger can't be said to be a desirable feeling, but it's essentially just your body's way of telling you that a need (that is, food) has not been met. Looking at it this way, you can try to understand rejection as a harmless feeling, just like hunger. Hunger is an undesirable feeling, but it's not often villainized. Without hunger, you wouldn't know that you need to eat. In the same way, rejection is an undesirable feeling, but it's not meant to harm you. On the contrary, it's meant to help you better provide for yourself by alerting you that a need has not been met. While hunger is a survival instinct that prevents you from starving, rejection is another survival instinct that prevents you from being alone. However, for people with social anxiety, their feelings of rejection often lead them to avoid social situations altogether, thus denying them any access to possible means of fulfilling their needs. To use the analogy of hunger once again, this would be like feeling your hunger yet becoming afraid of food and avoiding it.

Now that you understand rejection more, let's see how this may lead to social anxiety. Rejection may seem terrifying to you and increase your other fears that you're doing something wrong within social interactions. This is why some people with social anxiety may often interpret rejection in social situations even when it's not happening. Your fear of rejection may run so deep that you begin to perceive and misinterpret anything (even the most positive and sincere praise) as something negative and hurtful. These misinterpretations of rejection may falsely confirm to you that you've done something wrong in a social setting, further exacerbating your social anxiety. Another way that a fear of rejection may lead to social anxiety is by developing abandonment anxiety. This form of anxiety occurs when you feel like you're being rejected and even completely forgotten. This may stem from a sense of abandonment or neglect that you experienced when you were younger. Maybe your parents were very absent, or maybe one parent left. Whatever the cause of your abandonment anxiety, the end result is an intensification of your fear of rejection and social anxiety. You may believe that it was your fault that you were abandoned and that there's no hope for you to fix your actions or self that led to that rejection. This can lead you to overcompensate or try to redeem yourself with the person that rejected and abandoned you. Such actions often backfire as you may overstep certain boundaries, or you may be met with indifference, which will further ignite your sense of abandonment, fear of rejection, and social anxiety. Another way that your fear of rejection may increase your social anxiety is by increasing your anxiety response. When you're afraid of rejection, any social interaction that doesn't go smoothly or perfectly can have devastating effects on your mental state. As soon as you feel like you've been rejected, your desire to avoid that rejection will spike, and you will become anxious to fix things or avoid the same outcome in the future.

The last accompanying demon to social anxiety is shaming. As previously mentioned, humans are social animals. We take our cues from how those around us respond to us. As children, you may be shy, inhibited, and fearful around people you don't know too well as a defense against shaming. You test the waters and see what behaviors will earn you praise and what behaviors will earn you shame. If you were adequately encouraged, supported, and guided when you were young, you would have experienced more praise than shame growing up, and you will now be a balanced, confident person. As a teenager, you may have experienced a lot of self-consciousness and discomfort with yourself. You will have emphasized fitting in and having your own group of friends to avoid feeling ashamed. If you managed to make meaningful friendships that offered you care and support, you would have grown up to be a self-confident and mature person. But if you often felt ashamed as you didn't have a social group that you fit into, then you may have developed social anxiety. As an early adult, you're still strongly averse to shame, especially since now there are many new stressors that you may feel like you're not adequately prepared or skilled enough to deal with. You may feel that if you don't perform well in any area of your adult life, then you will be shamed by society, friends, and your family. This may lead you to develop severe anxiety and intense fears of being embarrassed in front of others. You may feel like this shame will make you seem weak, defective, or worthless in front of others. So shame can be understood as the feeling of being flawed or unacceptable. Though shame can have the adaptive function of guiding you to conform to the values, ethics, morals, and rules of your social environment, it can also be blown out of proportion and cause you to feel depressed, hopeless, and inadequate. The general areas in which you may feel shame are personal attractiveness, competence, intelligence, and lovability. The areas of your shame affect how you view and interact with the world. For example, if you're afraid of feeling shame in front of others, you may avoid social settings, thus contributing to your social anxiety.

Now you understand the various contributing factors of social anxiety. Try to reflect on what you've learned so far and determine which demons apply to you. In the next chapter, you will learn about how worry, panic, and fear exacerbate social anxiety.

Chapter Three

DEEP DIVE: WORRY, PANIC, AND FEAR

This chapter focuses on how worry, panic, and fear can make your anxiety worse. You will be given thorough explanations about how to best understand these emotions and why you must pay attention to them as you're healing from your social anxiety.

UNDERSTANDING WORRY

The first component of social anxiety is worry. This entails a specific way in which you think about the future that ultimately leaves you feeling apprehensive and anxious. When you worry, you can blur the lines between a real event and a hypothetical event. You will be swept away by your own chain of thoughts and images that are negative, unrealistic, and difficult to control. You may think that you're engaging in mental problem-solving by thinking about the future, but this mode of thinking about the future is not helpful to you at all, as you will typically become trapped by cyclical thinking or paranoia. When you worry about an issue whose outcome is uncertain, you may overemphasize the possibility of its negative outcome. Consequently, worry may often trigger your fear process and reactions. In certain cases, thinking about the future can be useful and productive. Humans have the astounding ability to mentally simulate events that are going to happen. You can think ahead and anticipate obstacles or problems, thus giving you the chance to plan ahead of time and effectively overcome the possible dangers or hardships that you will face. But there are productive and unproductive ways to think about the future. In the productive method of thinking, you will be realistic about the probable outcomes (not just the possible ones), spend your mental energy coming up with solutions, and maintain emotional balance throughout this process. This method of thinking ahead can be adaptive, flexible, reasonable, and help you achieve your goals. In contrast, worrying is an unproductive method of thinking where you're more unrealistic (thinking that the worst possible outcome will happen despite its improbability), experience more emotional distress, and spend your mental energy focusing on your negative emotions and thoughts rather than on coming up with solutions. This can make you feel uneasy and overly concerned about a situation or problem. Your mind and body become hyperactive as you overemphasize the possibilities of what might happen. Your mind will spiral into dark places and emotions while your body will react with fear and anxiety. This can be severely detrimental to your health in various ways.

Excessive worrying can damage your central nervous system as it can lead to long-term anxiety and panic attacks, which in turn, can cause your brain to release stress hormones more regularly. These stress hormones, which are only meant to be released once in a while whenever you're faced with a real threat, can cause symptoms of headaches, depression, or dizziness. Such symptoms may be experienced every time you feel anxious and stressed, as your brain will react by flooding your nervous system with hormones and chemicals that are supposed to help you respond to a real threat.

These hormones are useful when you're facing real danger and when you're only exposed to them for short periods of time (they should typically fade after the threat has been neutralized). However, when you excessively worry, your anxiety levels may remain high for longer periods of time, thus exposing you to these hormones in the long term. This prolonged exposure to stress hormones can become harmful to your physical health over time. For example, long-term exposure to stress hormones can lead to weight gain, difficulty swallowing, dizziness, dry mouth, increased heart rate, fatigue, difficulty concentrating, headaches, irritability, muscle aches, muscle tension, nervous energy, nausea, rapid breathing, sweating, trembling, twitching, and shortness of breath. When the stress hormones meant to fuel your body isn't used for physical activities (as is usually the case when you're excessively worrying), the chronic anxiety and increased levels of stress hormones can lead to serious physical consequences, such as a lowered immune system and digestive disorders (which you will learn more about below), muscle tension, short-term memory loss, heart attacks, or premature coronary artery disease. On the other hand, excessive worry can harm your cardiovascular system. Many of the physical symptoms of stress and anxiety have to do with your cardiovascular systems, such as increased heart rate, palpitations, and chest pain. Over time, you may even develop high blood pressure and heart disease (and if you already have heart disease, your anxiety may worsen it and increase your risk of coronary events). With the constant overstimulation of your cardiovascular system, there is bound to be some damage done to this system as time progresses. On a related note, your respiratory systems take a hit due to your excessive worrying. When you're anxious, you may begin to have rapid and shallow breaths. This can worsen your symptoms of asthma. And if you have chronic obstructive pulmonary disease, you may be more at risk of anxiety-related complications.

Next are your excretory and digestive systems. Anxiety can sometimes lead to stomach aches, diarrhea, nausea, and loss of appetite, which may then lead to gastric, and other digestive issues. Some people with anxiety even report that they develop irritable bowel syndrome after a bowel infection. This syndrome involves vomiting, diarrhea, or constipation. The connection may be that after having a bowel infection, people with anxiety become overly aware of their bowels and become anxious about its health and functioning. This extra stress and anxiety can exacerbate the physical symptoms of anxiety (such as diarrhea and stomach aches), eventually leading to the development of irritable bowel syndrome. Your immune system is also affected by your excessive worrying. When you worry about all the possible negative outcomes of the future, you can feel afraid and threatened, thus triggering your fight-or-flight response and releasing a cacophony of chemicals and hormones into your system. This can be useful in the short term by increasing your breathing rate and pulse to get more oxygen to your brain and muscles, thereby making you more alert and energized to face a threat. This prepares you to respond effectively and appropriately in an intense situation. Your immune system may even get a boost in the short term. With occasional worry, your body will return to normal functioning after the threat passes and your stress reduces. But with excessive worrying that leaves you feeling anxious for a long time, your body may not receive the signal to return to normal functioning. Your body will remain in a state of hypervigilance for too long, and over time this will weaken your immune system.

You will become more vulnerable to viral infections and frequent colds or fevers. Other negative effects of excessive worrying include headaches, muscle tension, depression, insomnia, social isolation, flashbacks (where you involuntarily relive a traumatic experience over and over), mood swings, irritability, sadness, or nightmares about the topic of your worry. With so many adverse effects, it only follows that you must be warier of your excessive worrying while you're trying to treat your social anxiety.

UNDERSTANDING PANIC

The next component of social anxiety is panic. Often, anxiety disorders can also lead to panic disorder (another anxiety disorder where you have frequent and sudden attacks of panic or fear). Though it's perfectly natural to experience panic sometimes in response to stressful or threatening circumstances, people with panic disorder experience panic regularly and at any time, regardless of whether or not there's a stressful or threatening event. One symptom of panic disorder is anxiety (this can range from worry to fear to panic; panic is the most severe expression of anxiety). As with social anxiety, you may start to avoid certain places and events for fear that they will trigger your panic. This will cause you to live in fear and to live in fear of fear, thus adding to your sense of panic and increasing the emotional distress you may feel. Another symptom of panic disorder is panic attacks. These attacks can come on very quickly and suddenly, for no apparent reason. When you have a panic attack, you will feel a rush of intense, uncomfortable, and scary mental and physical symptoms. Panic attacks can be paralyzing and distressing. The symptoms include racing heartbeat, feeling faint, chest pain, sweating, nausea, shortness of breath, hot flushes, trembling, chills, weakness in your limbs, a choking sensation, numbness, dizziness, dry mouth, ringing in your ears, a need to go to the toilet, feelings of dread or fear or dying, tingling in your feelings, stomach issues, and dissociation (where you feel like you're not connected to your body). Most panic attacks occur for about five to 20 minutes, though it varies on a case-to-case basis. The frequency of your panic attacks will also vary depending on how severe your panic disorder is. Some people have panic attacks a few times a month, while others have them several times a week. Panic attacks can feel threatening and dangerous, but they won't actually cause you physical harm. Nonetheless, it's important that you understand the symptoms of a panic attack so that you can know when you're experiencing one and when you're not. For example, sometimes you may think that you're having a panic attack, but you may just be having a racing heartbeat or extremely low blood pressure.

Now that you understand panic disorder let's explore how it's different compared to anxiety. Though anxiety can lead to panic disorder and panic is a component of anxiety, panic disorder is a different issue compared to social anxiety. The first difference is the fear and avoidance you feel. People with panic disorder may often fear the physical symptoms of their panic attacks and, over time, feel safer from these attacks by staying within certain areas (that is, their self-determined safe zones). Sometimes, this fear of their panic attacks may develop and worsen to a point where they can't leave their safe zones without feeling intense fear. Meanwhile, social anxiety involves fears of being the center of attention, being criticized, or behaving in ways that would embarrass them in front of others. People with social anxiety typically fear public humiliation and the general discomfort they feel in social settings. These fears can develop and worsen to a point where the individual avoids public and social interactions. So though both panic disorder and social anxiety lead to avoidance, the cause of this avoidance differs in that people with panic disorder fear their panic attacks while people with social anxiety fear social rejection and humiliation. The next difference between these two disorders is their symptoms. Panic disorder involves recurring panic attacks that can happen suddenly, for no reason, and without warning. So the symptoms of panic disorder, in relation to panic attacks, are mostly physical. For example, they were shaking, had heart palpitations, and had difficulty breathing. These physical effects can make you feel like you're in real danger. You may worry that you're having a heart attack, losing control of your own body, or even going insane. The symptoms of social anxiety differ in various ways. Though the physical symptoms are similar (sweating, trembling, shortness of breath, and so on), these symptoms are only brought on when you think about public or social interactions and the possible negative outcomes. While the physical symptoms of panic disorder can come for no reason and without warning, the physical symptoms of social anxiety only come when you're worrying and panicking about social events. Social anxiety also involves other symptoms that aren't necessarily included in panic disorder: for example, low self-esteem, low self-confidence, and low self-worth. Lastly, another difference between social anxiety and panic disorder are their reactions to social interactions. People with panic disorder often feel ashamed or embarrassed about letting others witness their panic attacks. They may feel lonely since they feel like they need to keep their panic and panic attacks a secret from others. However, they still typically enjoy social interactions and can benefit substantially from proper social support. Their trusted friends and family members can help and support them. On the other hand, people with social anxiety also experience a lot of loneliness, but they have a harder time with social interactions. Any social interaction may cause them to feel overwhelming anxiety, so they may be more closed off from the help and support of their loved ones.

Be it panic or social anxiety; it remains that you must address these issues even as adults. Adulthood is an emotional and challenging time as you gain more independence, search for your identity, and juggle your everyday responsibilities (such as school, work, familial duties, and relationships). You will also go through new transitions and experiences and gain more duties (such as becoming financially stable, getting a reputable job, or getting into a good university). In addition, your use of social media may negatively impact your mental health as it can build an unrealistic, idealized picture of people and their lives. As you're struggling with adulthood, you may feel even more pressure as you compare your life to that of others on social media who all seem to be doing better than you. This can damage your self-esteem, self-worth, or body image, leading to even more anxiety or panic. You may try to overlook these emotions or suppress them because you feel like you don't have enough time to address these issues (considering all your various focuses, such as school, work, relationships, or your career). Another reason you may choose not to address your panic and anxiety is because of the common misconception that anxiety is not a real mental disorder. You may think that panic, worry, and anxiety are feelings that are totally normal and controllable. This is true if you only experience these emotions in moderation. But when you have an anxiety disorder, you will feel these emotions intensely and disproportionately almost every day for months or years. Anxiety disorder and panic disorder are not things that will go away on their own. Like any other illness, you must treat them, or they can worsen over time.

UNDERSTANDING FEAR

The last component of social anxiety is fear. This includes the fear of being laughed at, the fear of being ridiculed in public, the fear of not getting a positive reaction or positive attention, and the fear of rejection in social circles. You will fear not being liked, being abandoned, not fitting in, or being alone. All these fears can create low self-esteem, low self-confidence, shame, and guilt within you, and you will spend a lot of time and energy worrying about how others think about and perceive you. You may then begin to neglect your own needs to try to please others, allowing yourself to be taken advantage of. If you're not clear on whether or not fear is a significant component of your social anxiety, these are the signs that fear has a certain degree of control over you. You may often put the needs of others before your own (to get others to like you), feel uncomfortable speaking your mind, or be hesitant to express your opinions (for fear that you may say something unfavorable that others don't agree with). You may also struggle to set healthy boundaries, say no to others (for fear that they will like you less for doing so), and stay in unhealthy relationships for too long (for fear of being alone and due to your low self-esteem). Other signs that fear is a significant player in your social anxiety are that you are a people pleaser (in an effort to endear yourself to others); take on too many responsibilities (because you think that being helpful to others will make them like you more), or work too hard (because you think that excellence will make you more socially acceptable). You may even be afraid of failure (as you think this may lead to rejection, criticism, or ridicule) and tolerate poor treatment from others (as you think that speaking up and causing conflict will make others dislike you).

While it's normal to want to fit in and be accepted, you mustn't let your fears control your life. There are various negative effects that can come from this. Your personal and professional relationships may suffer as you put unrealistic expectations on others, become clingy, request constant reassurance, become jealous or suspicious, or compare yourself negatively to others. All these traits will create emotions and behaviors that put a strain on your relationships. Fear can negatively affect your career in other ways: You may miss out on good opportunities, not ask for pay increases, accept unrealistic workloads, not discuss necessary changes to work responsibilities, or remain stuck in your current position out of fear. You may also experience interview anxiety where you don't apply for the job that you want, dread the interview process, freeze during an interview, or struggle through an interview. Or on the next step where you land a new job, you may experience anxiety and fear toward this new job and thus remain in that position for too long even if it's not a good fit for you. This can hinder you from growing your career. Or if a job is a good fit for you, your fear may still ruin it for you. You may work too hard and for too long to try to prove yourself in your position as you're afraid of being publicly reprimanded or judged by others. Meanwhile, your fears can harm your relationships as you may become cold, distant, uncommunicative, jealous, insecure, and needy. You may fear social rejection so much that you push others away and don't allow them to get close to you, just to avoid the possibility that they reject you. This can hinder you from making deep and meaningful friendships. Or if you're in a romantic relationship and you fear rejection, you will never be able to feel secure or comfortable. You will constantly ask for reassurance and project your insecurities onto your partner. Eventually, this will put a strain on the relationship and your fears will form a self-fulfilling prophecy. This means that your fear of being rejected may cause you to act and behave in ways that lead to you being rejected.

The most relevant fear for social anxiety is the fear of rejection in social settings. You may fear this possibility immensely and thus avoid social gatherings or interactions, choosing instead to stay at home, stand against a wall, or avoid talking to others. This fear of being socially rejected can give rise to many other related fears, such as the fear of not knowing what to say, the fear of not having anything interesting to say, the fear of saying something stupid, the fear of forgetting someone's name, and the fear of feeling awkward in a conversation. As you can see, your fear of rejection can multiply into several other fears, thus increasing your experience of this emotion. Another type of fear you may experience is the fear of rejection in business. This can stop you from following your dreams, living up to your full potential, and helping others with your ideas and services. Next, there is also the fear of rejection in creativity. Your fears may make you hesitant to try something new or explore a creative avenue, thus stifling your creativity. You may hesitate to share your work with others or to ask for the help you need to hone your skills. This prevents you from improving and prevents others from giving you honest and constructive feedback on your work. Finally, there is the fear of rejection in new friendships. You may avoid putting yourself out there, meeting new people, or making deeper connections with others because you're afraid that they may eventually reject you, leave you, or hurt you. But making new friends requires a certain degree of vulnerability. You may think that avoiding making new friends keeps you safe from rejection and pain, but all it does is leave you lonely and isolated. This is why you must take special care to be aware of your fears within your social anxiety. Don't allow your fears to dictate your life.

WORKSHEETS TO HELP YOU COPE

On that note, let's begin working through some worksheets that can address your worry, panic, and fear. First, let's start with your worry. When you worry, you tend to imagine the worst possible outcome, regardless of their probabilities. Your worries are usually unrealistic and exaggerated outcomes that will never come true. But when you're worrying, it becomes hard to distinguish between what could happen and what will happen. This Worry Exploration Questions worksheet can help you consider your worries in relation to reality. You will ask yourself several Socratic questions that will lead you to explore the most likely outcomes for the situation that you're worried about. This can counteract your tendency to only imagine the worst possible outcomes. To do this worksheet, answer the following questions in this order:

- What are you worrying about? Identify the issue and be specific about what's occupying your thoughts. You can even include the possible negative outcomes you're thinking of that are causing you distress.
- What are some clues that your worry will not come true? Think of facts and evidence that go against your worries.
- If your worry doesn't come true, what

will probably happen instead? This opens up your mind to new possibilities and encourages you to consider things from a more realistic perspective.

- If your worry does come true, how will you handle it? Will you eventually be okay? Will it be the end of the world? These questions can help you realize that your worries may be overemphasized and exaggerated. They can also increase your self-esteem as you will see that, no matter what happens, you can survive.
- After answering these questions, how have your worries changed? This question asks you to reflect on this worksheet so that you can be aware of how your thoughts are changing.

The next worksheet offers you coping skills to manage your excessive worrying. These techniques can distract you from your worries for a moment and help you manage your long-term anxiety. This worksheet simply offers you flashcards of possible coping skills that can help you ease your worry. The coping skills you will learn are:

- Stop and Listen: spend some time listening to the sounds around you. What can you notice? Are the noises loud or soft? Are there any interesting sounds that you've never noticed before? This can distract you from your worries and calm your mind so that you're more able to think rationally about your situation.
- Favorite Place: Think of a place that makes you feel happy, calm, and comfortable. This can be a real or imagined place. Create a visual picture in your mind of what this place looks like and imagine how good you feel when you're there.
- Journal: Write about your worries to explore them and make them seem more manageable. Ask yourself what you're worried about, what you do when you're worried, and what happened the last time you worried about something similar. These questions can help you gain some perspective on your situation.
- Deep Breaths: Breathe in slowly through your nose and hold the breath in your

lungs. After a few seconds, exhale and put your lips together like you're blowing through a straw. Do this 20 times to ground, center, and calm yourself.

- Draw Your Worry: This helps you creatively express and explore your emotions. Draw a picture of your worry. You may choose to draw what you look like when you're worried versus what you look like when you're calm, what you can do to stop worrying, and something that you're worried about.
- Write a Happy Ending: This skill can be useful for you if you like writing. Usually, when you worry, you imagine the worst-case scenario. Try to overturn this by writing about your worry and making the ending positive. Write about how you can solve this problem, relax, start to feel better, and decrease your worry.
- Listen to Music: Enjoy your favorite music to take your mind off what's worrying you. Try to focus on the instruments, lyrics, and voices in the song, or just allow yourself to be carried away by the song itself.

- Talk About It: Talking about your feelings can help you feel calmer and more in control. You can get started by filling in this sentence: "I feel worried when ..."
- Get Moving: When you worry, you often get lost in your internal world. Counteract this by getting more involved in the external world. Work out all your nervous energy by being active. One way to do this is to practice a hobby.

Next, let's discuss some worksheets to help you with your panic. The first worksheet aims to help you understand your panic attacks, as this will bring you closer to getting rid of them for good. After answering the questions in this worksheet, you will have a better overview of your panic attacks and how they fit into the rest of your life. Take some time to reflect as you answer these questions:

- How often do your panic attacks occur?
- How long do your panic attacks usually last?
- Rate the severity of the symptoms of your panic attacks where 1 is "I don't

have this symptom at all" and 10 is "I experience this symptom intensely."

Below is a list of symptoms for you to rate in this way:

- Palpitations, pounding heart, or accelerated heart rate ___
- Sweating ___
- Trembling or shaking ___
- Shortness of breath or feeling smothered ___
- Feelings of choking ___
- Chest pain or discomfort ___
- Nausea or abdominal pain ___
- Dizziness, unsteadiness, light-headedness, or faintness ___
- Cold or hot flushes ___
- Numbness or tingling ___
- Feeling of unreality or like you're going insane ___
- Feelings of dissociation or being detached from yourself ___
- Fear of losing control ___
- Fear of having a heart attack or dying ___
- Do you experience fear of places or situations where getting help or escape

might be difficult, such as in a crowd or on a bridge?

- Do you feel unable to travel without someone with you?
- Are you constantly worried about having another panic attack?
- Are you constantly worried about having a heart attack or going crazy?
- Have you changed your habits and behaviors to try to avoid having another panic attack?
- Have you experienced changes in your sleeping or eating habits?
- Do you feel sad, depressed, or disinterested in life for at least four days a week?
- Do you feel worthless or guilty more often than not?
- In the last year, has the use of drugs or alcohol caused you to fail to fulfill your responsibilities at work or school or in your family or relationships?
- During the last year, has the use of drugs or alcohol caused you to be in dangerous situations?
- During the last year, has your use of

drugs or alcohol persisted despite the problems they cause for you and your loved ones?
- Describe your typical panic attack in as much detail as possible.
- What usually helps your panic attacks go away?
- How do your panic attacks keep you from living life to its fullest? How have your panic attacks affected your quality of life?
- How will your life change when you no longer have panic attacks?

Answering these questions can help you understand yourself more. The self-reflection these questions encourage can lead to meaningful insights that can nurture your self-improvement and self-healing.

Another worksheet for panic focuses on grounding techniques. These are a set of tools that can help you stay in the present during panic attacks or episodes of intense anxiety. When you stay in the present moment, you help yourself to feel safe and in control. These are amazing benefits, and they can be achieved easily through simple grounding techniques. Just focus on some aspects of the physical world rather than allowing yourself to be swept up by your thoughts and emotions. By focusing on the physical world, you focus on the present rather than the past or future. Below are some grounding techniques. Try them all and make a note of which ones are most effective and helpful for you:

- run cool water over your hands
- grab onto your chair as tightly as you can
- touch various objects around you (such as your pen, keys, clothes, or the wall)
- dig your heels into the floor and notice the tension as you do this
- notice your body (such as the weight of your body in your seat, your toes in your socks and shoes, or the feel of the chair against your back)
- stretch
- clench and release your fists
- walk slowly, noticing every step you take
- breathe slowly, noticing every breath you take

- eat something and describe the flavors to yourself

Moving onto fear, this worksheet brings you through an exposure ladder where you slowly expose yourself to the things you fear, gradually lessening your fear response to them. The first step is to grade your fear items. List down all the things you fear, categorize them into relevant groups, and rate how much you fear each item on a scale of one to 10. Think about all the activities you fear in relation to a specific phobia and rate each one. Then, arrange your fear items in ascending order. The second step is to start exposing yourself to these items. Start with the simplest one—the item that was ranked the lowest. Stay in that situation for a prolonged period of time until the anxiety and fear you initially felt drops by about 50%. Once you conquer this item, work your way up your fear ladder by moving on to the second lowest rated item. The third step is to repeat your exposure activities. Consistently expose yourself to one situation until your fear rating at the start of the exposure can be ranked as a four or lower. Some things to remember while doing this exercise is to do it without trying to distract yourself from the fear you feel. Instead, allow yourself to feel the fear. This will be uncomfortable, but it will help you overcome your fear quicker. If the fear you feel is too intense, it's okay to drop down on your exposure ladder and try exposing yourself to something with a lower rating. This is how you can overcome your fears. In the next chapter, you will begin to learn about cognitive behavioral therapy and how it can help you with your social anxiety.

Chapter Four

UNDERSTANDING WHY COGNITIVE BEHAVIORAL THERAPY IS WORTH IT

This chapter will introduce you to cognitive behavioral therapy (CBT) as an approach to overcoming social anxiety. You will be taught what CBT is, how it works, and how it is recommended to help treat social anxiety.

UNDERSTANDING CBT

CBT is a psychotherapeutic treatment that can help you learn how to identify and change the distressing, destructive, and disturbing thought patterns you have that have an adverse effect on your actions and emotions. To achieve this, CBT combines cognitive therapy with behavior therapy. This means that through CBT, you will be led to identify your faulty or maladaptive forms of thinking, emotional reactions, or behavior (the cognitive therapy part) and then substitute them with more desirable and effective patterns of thought, reactions, and habits. Overall, CBT focuses on altering your automatic negative thoughts, which can contribute to or exacerbate your emotional distress, depression, panic, and anxiety. These thoughts are usually spontaneous, involuntary, unconscious, hard to control and have a detrimental effect on your mood. The main goal of CBT is to help you become more aware of these thoughts, identify them, challenge them, and replace them with more objective, helpful, and realistic thoughts. There are various types of CBT that use a range of techniques and approaches to address your thoughts, actions, and emotions. Some of these forms of CBT require a therapist, while others can be self-administered as self-care practices. A few types of CBT are:

- Cognitive therapy: This centers on identifying and changing your inaccurate, faulty, and distorted thought patterns, habits, and emotional reactions.

- Dialectical behavior therapy: This therapy addresses your disturbing, distressing, and destructive thoughts and habits while incorporating treatment methods such as mindfulness and emotional regulation.
- Multimodal therapy: This therapy suggests that psychological issues must be treated by addressing seven distinct but interlinking modalities, which are behavior, sensation, affect, imagery, cognition, interpersonal factors, and drug or biological considerations.
- Rational emotive behavior therapy: This therapy involves identifying your irrational beliefs, actively challenging them, and learning how to recognize and change your thought patterns.

All these various forms of CBT take nuanced approaches to treating patients, but they all fundamentally work to address your underlying thought patterns that are causing you psychological distress and replace them with better-coping strategies. To achieve this, CBT (in all its forms) uses a few set techniques in its treatment methods.

It's not enough to identify your thought patterns; you still need a wide range of strategies to eventually overcome these patterns. Here are a few techniques used in CBT:

- Identifying negative thoughts: The first step in CBT is to learn what thoughts, feelings, and situations are leading you to exhibit maladaptive and unhealthy behaviors. This process can be difficult, especially if you struggle with self-reflection and introspection. But it is a worthwhile journey as taking the time to identify your negative and unhelpful thoughts can lead to self-discovery and certain insights that are vital to your healing process.
- Practicing new skills: In therapy, and especially in CBT, you will be taught new skills that can help you better navigate your reality and real-world situations. You may find it hard to do certain everyday tasks and thus rely on maladaptive behaviors. For example, you may find it hard to go to the supermarket if it's crowded as you're

worried you may make a fool of yourself in front of a lot of strangers. This leads to the maladaptive habit of avoiding the supermarket or only going at odd hours when fewer people will be there. With CBT, you will be taught some skills that allow you to live your life unhindered.

- Goal setting: Setting goals can be important for your recovery process as this can help you make changes, improve your health and life, and provide you with tangible proof that you're making progress. Through CBT, you can build and strengthen your skills in setting goals. You will learn how to identify your goals and how to categorize them into short- or long-term goals. You will also learn how to set SMART (specific, measurable, attainable, relevant, and time-based) goals to increase your chances of achieving your goals.
- Problem-solving: Many times, you experience psychological distress because you're unsure of how to solve certain problems. Your life may be filled with many stressors that you're not sure

of how to deal with. With CBT, you will learn problem-solving skills that will teach you how to identify and solve problems, big or small. This can even help to reduce the negative impact of psychological and physical illnesses as you're more prepared to face adversity. The problem-solving skills in CBT usually involve five steps: Identify the problem, generate a list of potential solutions, evaluate the strengths and weaknesses of each potential solution, choose a solution, and implement the solution. This may sound too easy and unrealistic, but a therapist would be able to guide you through each step and help you feel more in control.

- Self-monitoring: This includes journaling, tracking your behaviors, symptoms, or experiences, and reflecting on these records. For example, for someone with social anxiety, you may find it helpful to keep track of your emotions and the outcomes whenever you're involved in a social situation. This can help you reflect on what you were worried would happen and what actually happened.

These are the techniques that you can learn through CBT. You can learn these techniques on your own and administer them on yourself. However, you can also benefit from having a therapist or mental health professional conduct CBT with you. If you choose to see a mental health professional for CBT, you will typically undergo four stages:

- Assessment stage: Where you and your therapist get to know each other. You talk about yourself and your background, and your therapist can use this information to form a treatment plan for you. This usually takes place in the first few sessions. Through the foundational information you provide, the therapist will be able to assess your mental state, provide a diagnosis, and estimate how long your treatment may take. Here, you will take some time to identify the troubling conditions that you've experienced so far in your life.

For example, divorce, anger, grief, or medical ailment. Then you and your therapist may spend some time excavating each of these issues to determine which of them are affecting you the most.

- Cognitive stage: This is where you and your therapist work together to explore and understand your thoughts. This may include discussing past events that have shaped your thinking or discussing the significant figures in your life that have affected you. Through introspection and reflection, you will develop an awareness of your emotions, thoughts, and beliefs about yourself, your past, and your surroundings. You will receive more clarity on how you perceive certain incidents in the past, how you interpret certain behaviors, and what you think about your own worth and personality. Only by detailing your thoughts and beliefs can you identify which are inaccurate or negative. And by identifying your negative thoughts, you can identify which ones are contributing to your issues. After identifying specific issues, you will break your problems down into separate parts (this can be done by keeping a journal where you write down your thoughts and behavioral patterns). Then you will work with your therapist to analyze your emotions, actions, and thoughts to discover if they are realistic or helpful. You will interrogate how your thoughts and emotions affect each other and you.

- Behavior stage: In this stage, you and your therapist work together to forge new ways of thinking, and you begin to apply these new thought patterns in your life, creating new behaviors and habits that are healthier and more helpful. You will begin to reshape your inaccurate and negative thoughts, learning how to differentiate between facts and emotions. You will practice certain changes in your daily life. These changes may include challenging upsetting thoughts when they crop up and replacing them with better, healthier ones or recognizing when you're about to engage in behavior that will only worsen your emotional state or situation and instead doing something that will actually help you. You may be given some homework between sessions to help you practice these skills and healthy thought processes. Then, at each session, you will inform your therapist of how you've put those changes into practice and what it felt like to do so. From this, your therapist will be better able to make other suggestions to help you.

- Learning stage: In this stage, you will work together with your therapist to ensure that the changes you've created so far are sustainable and permanent. You will learn skills to deal with or prevent relapses. You will learn how to use the principles of CBT and apply them in your future situations. This way, you don't need to rely on therapy forever but can learn to be independent.

These four stages are not always separate. They can overlap and get mixed up, but throughout the entire CBT process, these stages will be aimed at helping you create a better, happier, more fulfilling life for yourself. Now that you know the stages and techniques of CBT let's further deepen your understanding of this therapy by exploring the characteristics of CBT. CBT is:

- pragmatic, as it can help you identify specific problems and then tries to help you solve them
- highly structured, as you will hone in on specific issues and set specific goals for yourself to achieve
- focused on current problems, as you will mainly concentrate on how you think and act now rather than focusing on resolving past issues
- collaborative, as your therapist won't tell you what to do but rather work with you and lead you to find your own solutions to your own problems

Finally, let's discover the pros and cons of CBT. The pros include the fact that CBT can be as effective as medicine in treating certain mental health issues, that CBT may even help in cases where medicine alone has not been effective, that

CBT can be completed in a relatively short period of time (the end goal of CBT is to have you become self-sufficient and prepared to take care of yourself in the long term), that CBT is highly structured, that it teaches you practical and helpful skills that can be applied in your everyday life, and that CBT continues to benefit you even after treatment has finished. Meanwhile, the cons of CBT are that you must commit yourself to the process to benefit from it fully, you must attend regular sessions of CBT and do homework in between the sessions (this can take up a lot of time and energy), it involves confronting your anxieties, fears, and worries (this can be uncomfortable but in the end, it is a worthwhile endeavor), and it focuses on the present without addressing or solving wider problems in systems or families or your past that may be harming your mental health. Hopefully, by now you have a rich and balanced understanding of what CBT is and what it entails. Now, let's learn why CBT is recommended for people with social anxiety.

WHY CBT IS RECOMMENDED FOR YOU

CBT can be used to treat a wide range of psychological issues. Many people prefer this form of psychotherapy as it can help you quickly identify your current problem and provide you with the relevant skills and strategies to cope with your life's challenges. And CBT generally needs fewer sessions compared to other forms of treatment as it is done in a structured and effective way. CBT equips you with various tools to address your emotional distress. For example, it can help you manage the symptoms of your mental illness, prevent any relapses once you've made progress, treat mental illnesses that aren't suitable to be treated by medication and learn techniques for coping with the stressors in your life. It can also identify ways to manage your intense emotions, resolve relationship conflicts, build better communication skills, cope with grief and loss, overcome emotional trauma (possibly related to abuse or violence), cope with medical illnesses, and manage chronic physical pains and symptoms. These are simply the general benefits that you stand to gain from CBT. Therefore, CBT is appropriate for treating various mental health disorders, such as depression, anxiety disorders, phobias, post-traumatic stress disorder, sleep disorder, eating disorders, obsessive-compulsive disorder, substance use disorder, bipolar disorder, schizophrenia, and sexual disorders.

But to get more specific, CBT works wonders for people with social anxiety. You will be led to analyze your thoughts, behaviors, and emotions. This means that you will identify what in your life is driving your feelings of self-consciousness and low self-confidence in order to reduce the physical symptoms you experience. CBT will help you recognize and reframe your distorted thought patterns and help you find various healthy ways to cope with social anxiety symptoms before and during a symptomatic episode. How you think about social situations and settings will influence how you feel and consequently act. So by challenging the thoughts, perspectives, and ideologies that shape how you think about social situations and settings and lead to maladaptive, unhealthy behavior, you can improve your mental state, mood, and habits. You will be able to see your life from a different angle and achieve a clarity of thought that will lead to better, more functional behavior. There are a few common CBT techniques used for social anxiety that can reduce the frequency and intensity of your symptoms. The specific techniques that will work best for you will vary depending on your unique symptoms, thoughts, and situations. Common symptoms of social anxiety caused by negative beliefs and feelings about yourself include not making eye contact, going to extreme lengths to avoid conversations, experiencing physical symptoms of anxiety, or agreeing with everyone (to avoid annoying others or to exit a conversation as soon as possible). In response to these symptoms, a therapist will likely use some of the following techniques to help you understand, deal with, and recover from your social anxiety:

- Challenging all-or-nothing thinking. This is a common technique that addresses a prevalent thinking error. People who tend to think in a linear way (that there's only one way to achieve a certain outcome or that things are either this or that) are usually less likely to achieve happiness and fulfillment compared to those who can think more openly and flexibly. With all-or-nothing thinking, you leave no room for gray areas, and this can be very limiting. Exploring the gray areas of life or the various ways to achieve a certain outcome can enhance your resilience and mental flexibility. This can prevent you from feeling stuck if an initial path doesn't work out the way you wanted.

- Attention training. This is a CBT technique where you learn how to shift your attention from yourself onto other people. People with social anxiety often live their lives trapped in their own minds, focusing on their mistakes, flaws, and emotions. While it's beneficial to be in touch with your thoughts, emotions, and behaviors, you may take this to the extreme and thus leave yourself tuned out from others. With CBT, you will learn to intentionally pay attention to what others are saying during a conversation rather than focusing on yourself and your aversion to being embarrassed. Shifting your focus in this way can help you to recognize that others aren't nearly as focused on you as you think they are. They aren't judging you, laughing at you, condemning you, or ridiculing you. Most of the time, they're probably absorbed in the conversation or in their own thoughts. This shift of focus can help you realize that what others are talking about has very little (or, in fact, nothing at all) to do with the worries and fears that you're usually preoccupied with.

- Psychological education. Through CBT, you will learn about the psychological aspects that contribute to your social anxiety. This can help you understand yourself and your condition better. This will teach you how certain thoughts lead to avoidance and how certain behaviors make your social anxiety worse. You will also learn how cognitive therapy can reduce your anxiety. Knowledge is important as you struggle to address your social anxiety. Knowing all about the problem and how to implement the solution can make your journey of self-healing a lot easier and more successful.
- Cognitive restructuring. This technique involves examining your negative

thoughts and thinking errors that arise during social situations: For example, all-or-nothing thinking, overgeneralizing, believing that everything is bound to fall apart, ignoring all the positive aspects and focusing only on the negatives, and believing that your emotions are accurate representations of the true reality (otherwise known as emotional reasoning). Once you're able to identify these things, you will be more able to recognize them faster in the future and challenge them. This is part of the process of restructuring the manner in which you interact with the world and with yourself.

There are many other psychological techniques and strategies involved in CBT, but these are the common ones used in treating social anxiety.

As a final word in this chapter, allow me to assure you that CBT is the most suitable and effective method of treating social anxiety. If you've tried the self-help techniques above (and to be expanded on in future chapters) and you're not seeing any noticeable changes, then you may need professional help. But it's completely feasible for you to make progress on your own. CBT is based on the theory that what you think affects how you feel, and how you feel affects how you act. So if you just change the way you think about social situations that give you anxiety, you will be able to change how you feel about them and how you act. You'll be able to feel less emotional distress and function better. Just remember to practice the CBT exercises and skills regularly. As you practice and prepare your mind, you will become more and more comfortable in the world, and your anxiety will lessen. In the next chapter, you will dive deeper into CBT and learn how to use its techniques to challenge your cognitive distortions.

Chapter Five

CHALLENGING COGNITIVE DISTORTIONS ABOUT YOUR ANXIETY

In this chapter, you will learn about the cognitive distortions that may exacerbate your symptoms of anxiety and learn how you can use positive psychology and cognitive behavioral therapy to challenge them.

TYPES OF COGNITIVE DISTORTIONS

The first thing you must do is learn how to differentiate and identify various cognitive distortions. Only then will you be able to challenge, question, and replace them. The problem with many people is that they're unaware of their cognitive distortions, so they simply believe in those erroneous ways of thinking and allow them to dictate and negatively influence their emotions and actions. This is why it's vital for you to learn about cognitive distortions now. Cognitive distortions are exaggerated thought patterns that are not based on facts. They can lead to maladaptive behavior and overly negative views. You may believe negative things about yourself, others, and the world that aren't necessarily true. Everyone is vulnerable to cognitive distortions; it's normal—especially when you're feeling down. But when you frequently engage in negative thoughts, your emotions and your mental health can deteriorate. But once you understand your cognitive distortions and are able to recognize when you're engaging in them, you will be able to reframe and redirect your thoughts, regaining control of your life. There are 15 common cognitive distortions that you may engage in. These include: filtering, polarization, overgeneralization, discounting the positive, jumping to conclusions, catastrophizing, personalization, control fallacies, the fallacy of fairness, blaming, 'should' statements, emotional reasoning, the fallacy of change, global labeling, and always being right. Below is an analysis of each of these fallacies. As you're reading this, try to examine yourself and see which distortions you identify with and which you tend to use in specific situations. So now, let's take a closer look at each cognitive distortion:

- Filtering: Mental filtering is when you have a selective perspective of situations. You will filter out all the positives and dwell instead on all the negatives. Even if there are more positive points to a situation or a person than negative points, you will still exclusively choose to focus on the negatives. For example, if your boss is reviewing your work and praising you for your hard work and positive results, but in the end, they make one small suggestion on how you can improve, you will zero in on that negative aspect. You will dwell on that suggestion the whole day and ignore all the positive things that were said.
- Polarization: This entails all-or-nothing thinking where you can only see things as black or white, leaving no space for middle ground or shades of gray. For example, when you get straight As you can think that you're a good, smart

student, but when you get one B on a test, you will think that you're a failure. You can only see yourself as a complete success or a complete failure. This can lead to unrealistic standards for yourself and others, which may set you up for failure and affect your relationships and motivation. For example, even if you're doing well in school, a single bad grade may lead you to conclude that you've totally destroyed your academic career and thus lower your motivation to keep trying. Or you may damage your relationships by missing out on the complexity of people and situations. If your family member is short with you, you may think that they hate you now, despite the fact that you have a positive, loving relationship with them.

- Overgeneralization: This is when you take a single, isolated, negative event and use it to perpetuate a pattern of loss and defeat. When you overgeneralize, you may use words like "always," "never," "everything," or "nothing." For example, if you speak up in a class discussion but your suggestions are not included or accepted, you may think to yourself that you never say the right thing or that you're never accepted or acknowledged. Overgeneralization also applies to your thoughts on the world and other situations. For example, if you're late for a meeting and keep meeting red lights on the way to work, you may think that nothing ever goes right for you.

- Discounting the positives: This cognitive distortion is similar to mental filtering. However, while filtering ignores the positives, this distortion notices the positives but immediately dismisses them as insignificant. For example, if someone compliments you, you may dismiss it as just trying to be nice. If your boss praises your work, you may discount it as something that anyone else would have been able to do. If your friends positively react to you, you may think it's simply because they haven't realized that you're no good.
- Jumping to conclusions: This is when you interpret a situation or event

negatively without any proof to support your conclusion. Then, you react to your own unsupported assumptions. For example, if your friend is in a bad mood one day, you don't ask them how they are but immediately assume that they're upset at you or that you did something wrong. As a result, you keep your distance from them. This may prevent you from reaching out to your friend and offering your help and support. The conclusions that you often jump to may be reflective of a persistent worry or negative thought of yours. For example, if you're insecure about your relationship, then anytime your partner seems upset, you will jump to the conclusion that they're upset at you or that they're losing interest in you.

- Catastrophizing: This is similar to the previous distortion, only this thinking error also involves jumping to the worst possible conclusion in every situation without considering the probability of that conclusion. This cognitive distortion uses a lot of *what if* questions. For example, *what if* your friends are all just pretending to be nice to you, *what if* your family member didn't call because they were in an accident, *what if* your friend hasn't arrived yet because they don't want to spend time with you, *what if* this person ends up betraying and abandoning you. And catastrophizing can often build off of one event. For example, what if your alarm doesn't work, what if you're late for this important meeting, what if you get fired. Small events or worries can lead to huge, life-threatening questions.

- Personalization: This is when you take everything too personally. You may believe that you're to blame for things that are actually completely or partially out of your control. This can lead you to feel guilty and to beat yourself up without considering all the factors involved. For example, if your friend gets into a small accident, you blame yourself for not offering to drive them. Or, if your friends are talking about traits that they don't like in people, you assume that their words are personal attacks on your character.

- Control fallacies: This distortion refers to the illusions, misconceptions, or errors that you may have regarding control. This can occur in two ways: You may feel responsible for everything in your life and in the lives of others, or you may feel like you have no control whatsoever over anything in your life. For the first type, you believe that your actions and presence can affect or control every aspect of your own life and the lives of others. For example, you may think that you have the sole power to make everyone else happy or unhappy, so you may think that their emotions, moods, and behaviors are all directly or indirectly influenced by your behaviors. This may also make you think that you're responsible for their emotions and actions. The second type of control fallacy leads you to place all responsibility and control of your behavior on others or external circumstances. For example, if you couldn't complete your homework or a work report in time, you may think that it isn't your fault and it wasn't in your control as you are being overworked by others.

- Fallacy of fairness: This refers to the habit of measuring every action and circumstance on a scale of fairness. This can lead you to resent whoever doesn't agree with your assessment and value of fairness. You may believe that you know what's fair and what isn't and that others should subscribe to your views. This may lead to conflicts with certain people and events as you feel like they're not abiding by your views and values of fairness. You may not realize that fairness is not often absolute and often self-serving. For example, you may think that it's fair to expect affection and attention from your partner since you've spent so long preparing their dinner. But they may think that it's fair to relax after a long and tiring day at work.
- Blaming: This fallacy leads you to make others responsible for how you think or

feel. People with this distortion often use the phrase "You *made me...*" For example, *you made me* feel bad, *you made me* jealous, *you made me* insecure, and so on. But even when others engage in unhealthy and hurtful behaviors, you're still in control of how you feel. They're not responsible for your reactions. This distortion may make you believe that others have more power over you than they actually do. The truth is that you have more power over your own self than anyone else does. For example, if your partner comments negatively on your outfit, you may tell them that they made you feel bad about yourself and feel upset for the whole day.

- Should statements: Should statements are subjective and rigid rules that you set for others and yourself without considering any other aspects of a situation. You fixate on how things should be a certain way and leave no room for exceptions. For example, you may think that people should always be on time, that you should always make people laugh, or that independent people should never ask for help. A common *should* statement includes thinking that you *should be* better. When things don't measure up to your rigid expectations, you may feel guilty, frustrated, or disappointed.

- Emotional reasoning: This leads you to believe that your emotions are accurate interpretations and reflections of reality. If you feel a certain way about an event, then you believe that it must be a fact. For example, if you feel like you embarrassed yourself at a party, you may think that you really did embarrass yourself without considering what actually happened. Or if you feel like your friends are mad at you, you may use this emotion as a fact that they are. Or, if you feel anxious about the future, you may believe that something bad is really going to happen.
- Fallacy of change: This fallacy occurs when you expect others to change their ways and their habits to suit your needs and expectations. You may think that if

you pressure them enough, they're bound to change for you. For example, if your partner is very sociable and values their friends, but you want them to spend more time with you and focus more on you, you may act out every time they go out with their friends and think that eventually, they will change for you.

- Global labeling: This involves taking a single trait or attribute and turning it into an absolute. Labels are typically negative and extreme, so this distortion often leads you to judge yourself and others based on isolated events. For example, if you get a bad grade one time, you may label yourself as useless. Or, if you see your friend using makeup once, you may label them as shallow. This is an extreme form of overgeneralization that can lead you to harshly judge yourself and others without considering the context. This can make your views of yourself and others overly critical and unrealistic, and it can harm your relationships. When you label someone, you judge them negatively and may, in turn, begin to treat them worse. And when you label yourself, you may harm your own self-esteem and confidence, leading you to feel even more self-conscious, anxious, and insecure.

- Always being right: This distortion refers to your desire to always be right, to the point where you disregard facts, evidence, and the feelings of others. You may mistake your opinions as facts and then go to great lengths to show that you're right.

POSITIVE PSYCHOLOGY

Now that you understand how cognitive distortions may be affecting your life let's discover how you can fix this. One avenue you can explore is positive psychology. This field helps you become happier, more fulfilled, and relaxed by helping you understand how to be more optimistic, resilient, and positive. You will study happiness and how you can make your life more fulfilling. By recognizing your strengths, noticing more of your positive emotions and experiences, and learning how to utilize your skills and talents to your advantage, you can increase your well-being, overall happiness, and mental health. There are three levels of positive psychology: The subjective level, which focuses on happiness, optimism, and well-being in your daily life; the individual level, which combines the previous level with qualities and traits that make you more well-rounded, such as love, courage, and forgiveness; and the group level that focuses on positive interactions with your friends, family, and community, including traits such as altruism, social responsibility, and reciprocity.

There are many ways to incorporate positive psychology into your everyday life to become happier and more satisfied. Firstly, try to practice *gratitude*. This is a popular positive psychology lesson that can help you experience more positive emotions, express more kindness and compassion, sleep better, have better immune systems, and feel more alive. To help you practice gratitude, try to keep a gratitude journal where you record what you're thankful for every day. Or you can take pictures of the things that you're grateful for and look through them later. Or you could volunteer, write thank you notes, spend time in nature, or call a friend. The second positive psychology trait you can develop is humor. Having a good sense of humor can shift your focus from the sad, depressing things in life to the fun, uplifting, hopeful parts of life. Laughter has actually been shown to reduce physical pain, reduce stress, improve your mood, and improve resiliency. On a related note, try to smile more. Smiling can have the same effects as laughing, where your happiness and emotional well-being improve while your stress and anxiety decrease. Another way to practice positive psychology is to visualize success. Imagine yourself acting in new, healthier ways. This can create a mental picture for yourself that you can then try to emulate. Having a visual representation of success can even strengthen your confidence that you can achieve it and reinforce optimistic, positive thoughts. To visualize success, find a peaceful place where you can sit, relax your body, and close your eyes. Then, paint a detailed mental picture of whatever success you want to achieve, whether that's speaking confidently in front of others or attending a party. Consider all the details, from your voice to your posture to your self-talk. If you're having trouble visualizing a specific scene, try instead to visualize a desired state of mind, such as peace, relaxation, contentment, or confidence. Imagine a comfortable, pleasant, safe place that you associate with that desired mood. Use all your senses to paint this picture.

Another important positive psychology practice is *self-compassion*. You may find this helpful if you're often too hard on yourself, too judgmental and critical of yourself, and fixated on all your faults and imperfections. Such attitudes train you to focus on the negatives, damaging your confidence and self-esteem. You may also be less able to enjoy the positive experiences and events in your life. Self-compassion can be an antidote for all this. When you treat yourself with kindness, you allow yourself to live with your imperfections. One way to practice self-compassion is positive self-touch, such as giving yourself a hug. Or you can use compassionate self-talk where you acknowledge your mistakes, allow yourself to atone for those mistakes, and forgive yourself. Next, you can notice what you need and provide it for yourself. If you're hungry, eat a healthy snack. If you're tired, give yourself a break. Lastly, remember to anticipate, savor, and remember. The first step of this is to anticipate: Think about an upcoming enjoyable event and anticipate the joy it will bring you. Actively choose to focus on the joy and excitement that is available to you in your life. Next, savor your happiness and fully engage in your present. Life can often feel rushed, so remember to slow down and fully appreciate the good things you have. Finally, *remember*. Look back and reflect on all the good times you've had. Retell stories or look through old photos. Remembering your past joys can sharpen your memory and allow you to re-experience your past happiness.

CBT WORKSHEETS

Now let's see how CBT exercises can further help you to address your cognitive distortions. The first worksheet contains a list of questions that you can ask yourself to challenge your unwanted and unhelpful thoughts. These are the questions:

- What facts support this thought? What facts contradict it?
- What would the worst possible outcome be if this negative thought were true?
- Are you using past experiences to overgeneralize the current situation?
- How can you view this in a positive way?

- Will this matter one day from now? Or in a week or a month? How?
- Have you dealt with this scenario before? How did you deal with it?
- What advice would you give someone else in the same situation?
- What are you ready to accept about this situation or person?
- Are your thoughts helping you or hurting you in this scenario?
- Can you genuinely control this?
- What else may be influencing this situation, aside from yourself?
- Are you using "should" statements? If you are, are they truly necessary?

Another way to challenge your distortions is to understand where they come from. This way, you can replace them with more adaptive and rational thoughts to improve your mood, habits, and overall quality of life. Often, cognitive distortions arise when triggered by certain environmental factors, such as interactions with certain people or certain events in your life. For this worksheet draw a table with three columns. In the first column, list some of your common triggers. In the middle column, list the cognitive distortions that arise from those triggers. In the third column, write down some more positive, helpful, self-compassionate, and constructive thoughts that you can use to replace your negative thoughts. For example, in the first column you may write "I was late to class," in the second column you may write "I'm a hopeless student and I will fail my exams" (and try to identify which cognitive distortion describes your thoughts the best), and in the third column you may write "I can set my alarm earlier next time, so I have more time to get ready." This is a good way to challenge your cognitive distortions. In the next chapter, you will use CBT to improve your habits and behaviors.

Chapter Six

BEHAVIORAL THERAPY TO TAKE BACK CONTROL OF YOUR LIFE

In this chapter, you will use cognitive behavioral therapy to challenge the harmful behaviors that lead to social anxiety. You will also learn how to change your behavior to improve your social skills and take back control of your life.

CBT TO CHALLENGE YOUR SELF-CONSCIOUS BEHAVIOR

Your self-consciousness can breed various habits that heighten your social anxiety, cause you to avoid social situations, and lower your general quality of life. CBT can help you overcome such behavior by challenging them and asking you to practice thoughts and behaviors that contradict those negative habits. The first method of challenging your self-conscious behaviors is to practice compassion for others. Everyone you meet has their own internal lives, struggles, insecurities, and demons that they're facing. You are typically clueless about what others are going through. So try to practice compassion for others by having more empathy for the people you come across. This can prevent you from being overly critical or judgmental of others. And the less critical you are of others, the easier it will be for you to become less critical of yourself. People with social anxiety are often lacking in self-compassion, so by being more empathetic to others, you practice and develop your ability to express compassion. Once you heighten your capacity for compassion, it will be easier for you to apply it to yourself. Compassion can be hard to master for someone with social anxiety, so you must practice it every day. This will not only improve your relationships with others (as compassion leads you to be kinder, more patient, and more understanding), but it will also eventually improve your relationship with yourself.

The next tip to challenge your self-consciousness is to start to not care. One aspect of being self-conscious is that you will constantly wonder what others think of you. You may even catastrophize that they think very negatively of you, that they're making fun of you, or that they're judging you. These are common worries for someone who is self-conscious. This CBT tip advises you to take a step back and ask yourself, "so what?" Alternatively, you could say to yourself, "I don't care," or "whatever." These can be empowering statements that you can use every time you find yourself feeling self-conscious. If you continue to dismiss the situations that make you self-conscious, you may find your confidence growing. You will realize that it doesn't matter what others think of you, that it's not the end of the world if one person doesn't like you, and that your self-conscious thoughts are often baseless as your friends still like you and enjoy spending time with you. So pick a phrase that you can say to yourself every time you start to feel self-conscious. This phrase should remind you that the opinions of others can't affect your life and that your self-conscious thoughts don't rely on any evidence. Once you pick this phrase, be consistent in using it. This can help you defeat self-consciousness and gain confidence.

Moving on, it's good to try new things whenever you're feeling self-conscious. This may seem counterproductive as you may not do well at this new endeavor, thus making you feel even more self-conscious. But this is a good way to emphasize to yourself that mistakes are okay to make, that you don't need to be perfect all the time, and that you can always recover from a mistake. The list of mistakes that you can't recover from is actually quite short. Unless your mistake results in death, you can recover from almost anything. However, this may be hard to accept as you may have a fear of failure. This fear can keep you from trying new things, keep you stuck in your comfort zone, prevent you from taking chances, and generally prevent you from living your life. So take action against this fear and your self-consciousness by trying one new thing today. What's one thing you would usually be afraid of doing because you're scared of what people would think? Don't let fear hold you back anymore —go out and do it!

Something else that you'll learn more about in the next chapter is mindfulness meditation. This can help reduce your self-consciousness as you will be able to adopt a third-person perspective which can help you focus outwardly and make you more objective. When your focus is pointed outward rather than inward, you will feel less self-conscious as you're not focusing on yourself and how others may see you. Instead, you are focusing on those around you, allowing you to nurture your relationships with them (which can help reduce your social anxiety). You will learn various mindfulness exercises in the next chapter but for now, suffice it to say that mindfulness meditation involves sitting quietly, becoming aware of your thoughts, and accepting them without trying to judge or change them. A specific type of mindfulness meditation (which you will also learn more about in the next chapter) is breathing meditation. This meditation takes your physical body into account by using your breathing to improve your physical symptoms of anxiety. When you're anxious, you tend to breathe faster, causing your body to hyperventilate. Your heart will pump faster, providing more blood and oxygen (and hence more energy) to your muscles. This will make you tenser and on edge, ready to run away or fight a threat. But the thing about anxiety is that there's usually no real threat that you need to be protected against. So breathing meditation aims to counteract these physical symptoms of anxiety. There are various types of breathing meditations, but all of them aim to slow down your breathing so that your heart rate decreases, relaxing your body and, thus, your mind.

A good way to challenge your self-consciousness is to challenge your thoughts that are supporting and heightening your self-consciousness. As with your cognitive distortions, it's important to realize that thoughts only exist in your head—they are your beliefs, opinions, and views, but they aren't necessarily accurate or true. To challenge your negative thoughts, you can review the previous chapter to help you identify the thought patterns you have that are harming you and do the worksheets provided to help you challenge and replace those thoughts.

Further, try to do difficult things. This won't be fun in the beginning, but there are surely various things in your life that you didn't enjoy at first, then eventually came to appreciate. For example, making new friends: This can be extremely difficult for someone with social anxiety, so it definitely won't be fun at first. But this endeavor can lead to feelings of connection, satisfaction, fulfillment, and friendship, which are all worth the initial growing pains you will experience. You have to put in a bit of work and be willing to experience a bit of discomfort in order to put yourself out there, allow others to get to know you, and get closer to others. This won't be an easy process, but you must do it anyway, for things that are worthwhile. Remember to reward and congratulate yourself for doing difficult things. This can help you stay motivated and dedicated to the process. Over time, the difficult thing may become easier, and you will start to feel less self-conscious.

You can also try to put yourself in the shoes of others. This shifts your focus away from yourself and your self-conscious thoughts or feelings and makes you focus on how others may be feeling. One way to do this is to think of a time when you were in a similar position as they are in right now. For example, if you're at a party and someone introduces you to someone new then leaves you alone with them to make small talk, you may begin to feel self-conscious and get lost in your internal world. You may think that they view you as boring or worry that you have nothing to say. But this is a skewed, biased interpretation that's being fuelled by your self-consciousness. Try to use empathy to discover a more realistic, objective perspective. To this person, you're a stranger, a blank slate, someone they know nothing about. If you were in their shoes, what would you be thinking? A more realistic interpretation of the situation would be that you're both feeling awkward and wondering what to say. This can help you feel less self-conscious. Or, if they're being very talkative, a realistic interpretation would be that they are thinking how nice it is that they have someone to talk to. Another way to put yourself in the shoes of others is to become curious about others as an objective, third-party observer. This can make you more aware of the other person as you interact with them, allowing you to pick up on things that can help you understand them more. Watch what others do, listen to what others say, and think objectively and openly about the situation. So the next time you feel self-conscious, try to put yourself in the shoes of others so that you can gain a fairer, more objective view of the situation.

Another way to overcome self-consciousness is to realize the disadvantages of this emotion. When you're self-conscious, you often interpret situations in the worst light, making it hard for you to have an accurate read of social situations. You may also ignore the positive aspects of an interaction and only focus on the negatives. This can lead you to develop several cognitive distortions that, in turn, will increase your social anxiety. Once you recognize the harm of being self-conscious, you can practice switching perspectives. While being self-conscious is an inward focus, the method of being less self-conscious is an outward focus. You can try to master these two binary forms of focus by switching between them. This can help you learn the differences between the two and help you practice switching between them so that the next time you're inwardly focusing, you can more easily switch to the opposite mode of focus. So, whenever you're in a situation where you can simply observe things (for example, when you're on public transportation), try to first focus inwardly on yourself. Do this for about five minutes and think about how you feel. Then, switch to an outward focus by trying to notice the people around you and how they appear. After this, think about how you felt and what you noticed. This experiment can make you more aware of the direction of your attention, help you learn how to control it, and teach you how it makes you feel. You can even practice changing perspectives by smiling at others and talking to them. When in doubt, ask other people questions about themselves. This can break the ice and make the other person feel like you're interested in them.

CBT TO CHALLENGE YOUR INNER CRITIC

The next use for CBT that can benefit you is to challenge your inner critic. This CBT exercise consists of four steps you can slowly work through on your own time. The first step is to identify what your inner critic is telling you. Detail the negative things it is saying about you and acknowledge that these thoughts are separate from your real point of view. Remember that these thoughts are not an accurate reflection of reality—they are simply biased perspectives based on destructive attitudes and negative life experiences you've internalized as your personal point of view.

The second step is to separate yourself from your inner critic. Try to phrase your inner critic's words in the second person. For example, if you're thinking, *I am worthless. I can never get anything right. I'll never be successful*, try to write it down as "You are worthless. You can never get anything right. You'll never be successful." This can alienate your inner critic and make it a bit easier to see that they are not true statements. When you think in the first person, it's easy not to challenge these thoughts and to quickly accept them as fact. But when you think in the second person, these thoughts become the words of a hostile enemy and this makes it easier to challenge.

The third step involves responding to your inner critic. Once you've written down your negative thoughts in the second person, try to respond to them by writing down more realistic, compassionate, and objective evaluations of yourself. These statements should be written in the first person to help you internalize the positive, compassionate things you are saying about yourself. For example, in response to a negative thought that says *You are incompetent*, you can write, "I may struggle at certain things, like everyone else, but I am smart and competent in many ways." This will show you a kinder, more honest version of your inner voice and teach you how to apply this kindness to yourself.

The fourth and final step is to not act on your inner critic. Remember that your inner critic isn't objective and isn't working in your favor right now. So before you act, try to reflect and determine if that action is in line with your objective point of view, your goals, and who you want to be. By identifying your inner critic, separating yourself from it, and responding to it, you will enable yourself to achieve this step as your confidence will grow and your inner critic will become more understanding and compassionate.

CBT TO IMPROVE YOUR SOCIAL SKILLS

CBT doesn't only serve to get rid of your negative habits—it can also help you implement positive ones. For example, CBT can be used to improve your social skills. By giving you certain goals and changes to make in your life, CBT can help you improve how you interact with others. The first method is to improve your emotional intelligence. This plays into some of the methods of challenging your self-consciousness as it encourages you to put yourself in the shoes of others to try to imagine what they're going through and understand their feelings. This will help you understand their perspective, be more objective, and respond better to others. Conversely, another way to improve your social skills is to look inwards. This doesn't entail indulging in your inner world where your self-consciousness may take control. Rather, pay attention to your emotions, thoughts, actions, and triggers so that you can better control them while speaking with others. This requires you to balance your inward focus and outward focus. When you're feeling very self-conscious, shift your focus outward to help you understand others more and not dwell on your baseless negative thoughts. Once you're more settled, you can try to focus inward in a healthy way to help yourself respond better to others. To further this end, you can practice effective communication skills, such as active listening or open body language to demonstrate that you're paying attention and valuing what the other person is saying. This allows you to understand more of what they're trying to say and opens the door for more positive conversations. One way to practice effective communication is to ask more than you speak. Ask open-ended questions and allow others to respond. This is a good way to engage others. You can even try to give more compliments to others. This can make them feel happy and appreciated. However, make sure your compliments are sincere as there's no point in shallow flattery. To speak more on open body language and non-verbal communication, here are some tips to make your communication more effective: Face the person you're talking to (this can make it obvious that you're paying attention to them), be mindful of your tone (to avoid any misunderstandings and to remind yourself to be compassionate), make eye contact (this will increase the sense of connection between you two), and use your body language to show that you're present and attentive. In addition, uncross your arms and legs, sit up straight, relax your shoulders, and smile. On the other hand, you can simply fake it till you make it. Try acting more sociable, even if you don't feel like you are. Eventually, being social will become easier. Another way to help you be more sociable is to read the news. Many conversations revolve around what's happening in the world today so try to keep up to date so that you can chime in. As you're trying to be more sociable, don't let your emotions and thoughts get the best of you. You may feel insecure, self-conscious, and anxious or think that you will fail, but remember that these are just thoughts and feelings. They're not facts. You are not your thoughts. Take a deep breath and try to move past them. This can help you relax in a social situation. Another tip is to start small. Don't throw yourself into the deep end by attending a large social gathering that you don't feel prepared for. Start by practicing your conversation skills with trusted friends or family members. Or start by spending some time in a coffee shop practicing the skills you've learned so far. After this you can ease into larger social settings with more success.

Moving on, another way to improve your social skills is to not hide behind your phone. It has become acceptable to always be on your phone, even in social settings, but this may have negative effects on your social interactions. It's easy to use your phone to avoid social interactions. Sometimes you may even just pretend to be busy on your phone to avoid talking to someone. Or you may use it in a social setting to avoid feeling like an outcast. Whatever your reason, you may be using your phone to enable your symptoms of social anxiety. If you want the chance to connect with others, you need to first put away your phone. If you're on your phone, you signal to others that you don't want to be approached or that you're busy. This immediately cuts off any chance of interaction. So put away your phone and give others the chance to approach you. Or you can approach others. Make the first move and see how it goes. On a related note, try to do more things in person. You may rely on technology a bit too much to the point where it limits your human interaction. For example, you may have work meetings online, you may order delivery rather than going to eat at a restaurant, and you may have your groceries delivered rather than going to the store. These are all convenient adjustments in your life, but they do have the adverse effect of limiting your contact with others. And without regular human contact, your social skills may decrease. So, once in a while, try to do things in person. Go to the store to buy groceries, watch a movie in the cinema rather than streaming it, go to a bookstore rather than Amazon, and go to a cafe rather than ordering delivery.

Further, find structured social activities as this may make it easier for you to approach social encounters. Random social settings may confuse and overwhelm you. For example, if you're at a coffee shop, you may find it hard to strike up a conversation with a total stranger. So to ease the pressure, structured social activities can offer you a safer space to practice being social. For example, board game nights, sports, church groups, community work, or craft groups. Having a common activity in place gives you something to talk about if you're unsure in a conversation. These are all useful tips on how you can improve your social skills. In the next chapter, you will dive deeper into mindfulness and how it can help your social anxiety.

Chapter Seven

MINDFULNESS EXERCISES AND COPING SKILLS

You've learned a bit about mindfulness so far, but now you will explore more about mindfulness exercises you can use to overcome anxiety and how to benefit more fully from these exercises. Mindfulness is a useful coping strategy that you can use to replace your other, more unhealthy coping strategies that may have become habitual at this point.

UNHEALTHY COPING STRATEGIES TO AVOID

There are various unhealthy coping strategies that you may have inadvertently fallen into. For example, depending on drugs and alcohol, unhealthy eating habits, negative self-talk, isolation, catastrophizing, codependency, or aggression. These are all coping strategies that will damage your life, your happiness, and your relationships with others. So this section aims to simply warn you away from such unhealthy coping strategies. One of the most common coping strategies that is unhealthy is avoidance. You may simply avoid the issues that you don't want to face as this feels like an easier way to deal with them. But this doesn't solve the deeper issue, and eventually, that issue will surface once again in different or similar ways. In relation to this, some people may opt to sleep too much. This is much like avoiding your issues as sleeping is just another distraction that prevents you from addressing your problem and makes you feel better in the moment. Sleep is generally healthy, but if you sleep too much, then your physical body will deteriorate. An unhealthy coping strategy that deserves mention here, as well, is dependence on drugs or alcohol. This can be a slippery slope as these substances can give you confidence, boost your mood, numb your feelings, or reduce your negative thoughts that you actively try to avoid. These effects can feel terrific in the moment, but once you rely on these substances excessively, it can lead to severe health complications, addiction, risk of overdose, and death. Rather than open yourself up to these dangers, it's best to stay away from drugs and alcohol completely if you're using them as solutions to your social anxiety. Next, some people also use impulsive spending or retail therapy as a way to make themselves feel better. This can cultivate a lack of self-control within you, numb your risk assessment skills, and increase your impulsivity. This can then lead to financial problems, hoarding, or secrecy. Finally, you may even use overeating or undereating as a way to cope with your issues. This serves as a distraction from your emotional and mental distress. And needless to say, these habits can lead to significant physical trauma. So hopefully you're now more aware of the possible unhealthy coping strategies that you may fall into. This will make you more vigilant in avoiding them and more determined to replace them with healthier coping strategies.

THE BENEFITS OF MINDFULNESS MEDITATION

There's no doubt that mindfulness meditation is a healthy coping strategy, but how exactly does it help with social anxiety? In essence, meditation can help you make peace with your thoughts, learn to sit with them and accept them, and stop judging and fighting them. These are greatly beneficial effects for someone with social anxiety. This is because some of the symptoms of social anxiety include being too hard on yourself, worrying about embarrassing yourself, or assuming that others think the worst of you. Neutral, harmless thoughts (such as, *I'm nervous about going to this party*) can intensify and worsen until it damages your sense of self and self-esteem (such as by thinking, *There's something wrong with me*, or *Everyone hates me*). Such negative thoughts will lower your confidence and self-worth, making it hard for you to socialize in a healthy way. Despite your desire for connection, your lack of self-esteem and self-worth may convince you that you're bound to fail or be rejected, making it harder for you to forge connections with others. Having a negative self-image will also heighten your social anxiety as you will focus more on your flaws in social situations and interpret things negatively. All this happens because you believe in your thoughts (even if they're baseless) and allow them to control your actions and habits. But mindfulness meditation teaches you to approach your thoughts with curiosity rather than judgment. If you approach a negative thought with judgment, you may deem it undesirable and thus engage in avoidance behaviors or unhealthy coping strategies. Or you may judge it to be true and thus feel bad about yourself or avoid a certain social situation. But if you approach a negative thought with curiosity, you can interrogate it and challenge it from a calm, objective point of view. This can improve your self-image and reduce your symptoms of social anxiety.

Meditation can be extremely effective for social anxiety, especially when paired with CBT. Meditation can give you more power over your negative beliefs about yourself and help you nurture your self-compassion. These effects could reduce your defensiveness and guardedness in front of others and thus allow for more positive social interactions. Meditation can also lead you to be still, focused, and calm, reducing your worry, rumination, and anxiety. From a biological standpoint, meditation can even change your brain structure to improve your memory and learning while decreasing your sensitivity to anxiety and fear. Meditation has even proved effective for treating a wide range of conditions such as anxiety, depression, addiction, hypertension, heart disease, and chronic pain. And once you gain all these benefits from meditation, you will be more able to cope with life and make the most of your potential. Various issues that used to plague you and hold you back will fade into the background as you allow mindfulness to take charge of your life. You will even be able to play a fuller part in your family, friend groups, community, and workplace.

TIPS ON PRACTICING MINDFULNESS MEDITATION

Before you get into the specifics of practicing mindfulness meditation, let's go through some tips that can help you benefit more fully from the exercises and increase your success rate. The first thing to consider with mindfulness meditation is the length of practice. This meditation can be practiced daily or if you don't have a lot of time on your hands, a few times a week. Try not to do it too infrequently as this will reduce the benefits you gain from it. The more often you can afford to practice, the better. And the period for each session can be anywhere between a few minutes (as several miniature meditations done throughout the day) to 40 minutes (as longer, sustained sessions where you really focus on the exercise). You can help yourself practice these meditations throughout the day by placing reminders for yourself around your house or setting an alarm on your phone. You can even go for some meditation retreats to be led through meditation exercises. The next consideration to improve your meditation is the place and your posture. Find a place and posture that helps you be comfortable. You may choose to sit in a chair, lie on your bed, or sit on the floor. Though be careful not to pick a place so comfortable that you fall asleep. If you're sitting, don't slouch or curl into a position where you could fall asleep. Your posture should be relaxed but not slack. And be sure to wear clothes that are comfortable. Following this, be careful when you choose a time to meditate. Most people have a lot on their agendas, so be sure to pick a time when you will be free of distractions and stress. Maybe pick a time after your day's work so that you're not troubled by the workload you have in front of you. You can even silence your phone so that you won't be interrupted and tell your family and loved ones that you need a certain amount of time to be alone and undisturbed so that you can properly meditate.

Another tool to help you meditate is a

mindfulness meditation script. There are scripts available for different targeted problems, or there are basic scripts for general use. Most meditation scripts will follow the same pattern where you focus on your breath, sever yourself from analytical thoughts, and become more aware of your mind and body. You may experience some roadblocks when you first start out on your meditation journey, but you must remain determined and flexible to overcome any obstacles that come your way. You may find it hard to concentrate or hard to relax as your mind keeps racing when you try to slow down your thoughts. This can be disheartening, but keep practicing, and eventually, it will become easier. If you continue struggling, try making small adjustments to improve your chances of success. For example, meditate for a shorter amount of time, choose a simpler mantra to repeat and focus on, or learn how to notice your struggles without focusing on them. When you struggle, that's a sign to keep practicing rather than give up. Regular and consistent practice will help you strengthen your resolve to overcome your struggles and improve your meditation skills. Some extra tips to help you pull back your focus to your meditation are to gently remind yourself to return to the meditation (without being critical or judgmental of yourself), try a different location, choose a different time of day, or use a voice-recorded script.

MINDFULNESS MEDITATIONS TO DECREASE YOUR SOCIAL ANXIETY

Now, let's start learning some mindfulness meditations. The first one is simple, and it's called Sitting Meditation. To start you out on mindfulness meditation, try to do this exercise for only three to five minutes. The following are the steps to follow:

- Find a quiet and comfortable place to sit down and close your eyes.
- Try to focus on your breath. You don't need to clear your mind but simply allow your thoughts to come and go without judgment. Don't dwell on any thought but imagine your thoughts as a river flowing by. It's okay to become distracted—managing these distractions is an essential part of meditation. Simply bring yourself gently back to the exercise and allow yourself to feel your thoughts gliding by.

- As you become calmer and more centered, tune into your breath. Listen to the noises it makes. Feel your chest, lungs, and stomach expanding and contracting as you inhale and exhale. Take slow, deep breaths to accentuate these feelings.
- Now push your attention outward to notice your surroundings, though be careful not to dwell on any one image, person, or sound. If something you notice makes you anxious, don't focus on it but move your attention elsewhere. Loosely scan the room that you're in and allow everything to occur to you uniformly—don't let any single thing become more prominent. This way, your worries, and uncertainties cannot act out. Simply observe without judging, criticizing, or labeling. This can help you deal with the uncertainties of social anxiety in the future as you become better at zooming out, not focusing on your negative thoughts, and calmly taking everything in.

The next mindfulness meditation exercise is called Body Scan and it's slightly more complicated than the previous exercise. However, in addition to helping you cope with social anxiety, reducing your stress, and improving your emotional regulation, this exercise can also help you become more aware of your body in a non-judgmental way. The following are the steps to follow:

- Find a comfortable place to sit or lie down. Focus on your breathing and notice your bodily sensations as you breathe.
- Shift your attention to your toes. You can wiggle, tense, and relax your toes to help you fully place your attention there. Notice how your toes are feeling, every texture and movement that's occurring to them. No matter the sensation, remember not to judge anything that you're feeling. Simply accept it and move on.
- Once you've observed your toes for a while, move on and progressively do the same thing to every body part, working from your toes to your head. For

example, observe your toes, ankles, calves, knees, thighs, buttocks, lower back, stomach, chest, shoulders, arms, wrists, hands, fingers, neck, and head in that order.

Other than this, there are various breathing meditations that are available to you. One way you can conduct a breathing mindfulness meditation is simply to lengthen your exhales. Inhaling deeply is linked to the sympathetic nervous system (which controls your fight-or-flight response) and is thought to be able to help you calm down. But if you take too many deep breaths too quickly, this can actually stimulate the symptoms of hyperventilation, which decreases the amount of oxygen that is delivered to your brain. So it's equally important to lengthen your exhales. To practice prolonged exhales, push all the air out of your lungs, then just let your lungs naturally inhale more air. Then, focus on exhaling. Try to inhale for four seconds and exhale for six seconds. Do this exercise for two to five minutes. This can slow your heart rate, calm your body, and prevent you from inadvertently causing yourself to hyperventilate.

Abdomen Breathing is another form of

breathing mindfulness meditation. It involves breathing from your diaphragm (around your stomach) to reduce the amount of work that your body needs to do in order to breathe. To do this exercise, follow these steps:

- Lie down on the floor or sit in a comfortable position. Place one hand under your rib cage and place the other hand over your heart.
- Inhale and exhale through your nose. Notice how your stomach and chest move as you do this, if they move at all. See if you can isolate your breathing so that you bring the air deeper into your lungs. See if you can breathe in a way that moves your chest more than your stomach.
- Now try to do the opposite: Try to breathe in a way that moves your stomach more than your chest. To do this, try engaging your stomach muscles to push the air out as you exhale.

Another breathing mindfulness meditation exercise is Breath Focus. This incorporates deep breathing to reduce your anxiety. The following are the steps to follow:

- Sit in a comfortable position. Notice how you normally inhale and exhale.
- Mentally scan your body to notice any possible tension in your body (this recalls the skills you learned through the Body Scan meditation above).
- Take a slow, deep breath through your nose. Notice your abdomen and upper body moving. Exhale equally slowly (this is to prevent deep inhales done in quick succession, which can lead to hyperventilation). Do this for several minutes, paying attention to the movement of your physical body.
- You can choose a word to repeat to yourself (mentally or verbally) and to focus on as you exhale. This word can be "safe," or "calm," or anything else that works for you. Characterize your inhale as a gentle wave washing over you. Characterize your exhale as carrying all your negative thoughts and energy away from you.

Staying on breathing mindfulness meditations, Equal Breathing is a useful form where you focus on the specific lengths of your inhales and exhales to make them the same amount of time. In a comfortable position, count up to four seconds as you inhale through your nose, then count up to four seconds as you exhale. As you breathe, be mindful of your counting and of your physical sensations.

Lion's Breath is another interesting meditation that can help you calm your anxious thoughts and relax your mind. This exercise involves exhaling forcefully. To do this exercise, follow these steps:

- Get into a kneeling position by crossing your ankles and resting your weight on your feet. If this isn't comfortable for you, try to sit cross-legged. Place your hands on your knees with your fingers outstretched.
- Take a breath in through your nose.
- Breathe out from your mouth, vocalizing a certain sound, such as "ha." As you exhale, open your mouth as wide as you can and stick your tongue out, stretching it as far down as it can. Focus on the

middle of your forehead or the end of your nose as you exhale.

- Relax your face as you inhale. Repeat the inhale and exhale up to six times or as many times as you need.

Moving on from breathing meditations, there is also Progressive Muscle Relaxation, a mindfulness meditation meant to counteract your normal stress response (your fight-or-flight response). Anxiety often activates this response and doesn't allow it to fade, which can cause several negative physical symptoms, such as stiffness, soreness, and tension in your muscles. Relaxation techniques such as this can reverse these effects, relax your body, lower your heart rate, reduce muscle tension, and calm your mind. You may even gain awareness of how your physical state is affecting your emotional state. By relaxing your physical body, you may guide your mind to relax as well, making it easier for you to let go of your anxious thoughts and emotions. To conduct Progressive Muscle Relaxation, follow these steps:

- Sit in a comfortable position. You can

close your eyes if this helps you to concentrate.

- Breathe deeply through your nose, feeling your body expand and contract. Repeat three to five times.
- Squeeze one of your feet as hard as possible. Notice how tight the relevant muscles feel. Hold this tension for 10 seconds, then release it. Let your foot relax completely and release all tension. Let your foot go slack and notice how different and relaxed it now feels compared to before when you were clenching your foot.
- Repeat this method of increasing and releasing tension on every body part, working your way up from your feet to your face. For example, follow this order: legs, glutes, abdomen, back, hands, arms, shoulders, neck, and face. Repeat this method a few times in any area that feels particularly stiff. This can relieve your physical stress and calm your mind.
- Take a few more deep breaths and notice how calm and relaxed you now feel.

These are useful mindfulness meditation exercises that you can use to overcome your social anxiety. In the next chapter, you will receive a few more CBT exercises, positive psychology worksheets, and daily exercises to help you improve yourself.

Chapter Eight

CBT-BASED EXERCISES, POSITIVE PSYCHOLOGY EXERCISES, AND DAILY ACTIVITIES TO MAINTAIN AN ANXIETY-FREE LIFE

In this last chapter, you will be led through a few more CBT exercises, positive psychology exercises, and useful daily activities meant to maintain an anxiety-free life. These activities, worksheets, games, and daily practices can help you handle the social anxiety issues that crop up in your daily life.

CBT GAMES

One way to ease yourself into CBT is to make it into a game. There are various CBT games you can create to make it easier for you to acquire certain skills, such as emotional regulation, recognizing cognitive distortions, and effective communication.

One CBT game is Feelings Pictionary or Feelings Charades. This game can strengthen the connection you have with others, teach you more about yourself, and train you to express your emotions. You play this game by coming up with your own prompts, such as: Draw a feeling you had today, act out a coping skill, what's your favorite thing to do after work, how did it feel when that person was rude to you, how can your parents or friends best help you when you're upset, how does your body feel when you're having a panic attack, and other relevant questions. You can choose to draw these out or act them out. And it's not necessary to keep score; just keep guessing each other's depiction. You can even take some time each round to discuss what you've depicted and interpreted.

Another CBT game is Dice Prompts. This game helps you learn and practice coping skills, respond to prompts, and strengthen your relationship with others. Assign your own prompts to each number on the die. Then, simply roll and take turns answering. To make this game more extensive, you can use two dice. For the first die, create corresponding categories, such as: coping skills, cognitive distortions, expressions of appreciation, avoidance habits, safety habits, and so on. Then, for the second die, you can create corresponding prompts. This way, you'll have more prompts to answer to keep the game going for longer and to increase the benefits you can gain from this game.

If you have cards at home, you can even make your own therapy card game. The goals of this game can be to review coping skills, respond to prompts, and build rapport with others. Take a deck of playing cards and add your own prompts or activities to each card. You can customize this however you want. For example, you can make a therapy game out of Go Fish where, for each set you earn, you must answer a prompt. This combines therapy with a traditional, easy card game. Alternatively, you could just take turns drawing cards and following the prompts. Your prompts can ask you to list coping skills, act out cognitive distortions, and so on. You can keep score and allow whoever wins a game or scores a point to ask another player any question they want. And the rule is that the person being asked the question cannot get angry or respond negatively. You are allowed to choose not to answer if the person isn't comfortable sharing yet, but then the winner gets to ask another question.

This part of the game requires mutual respect and trust.

You can use anything you have nearby or any board games you have to help you practice CBT skills and knowledge. Just add a prompt or question to a function or play of the game. For example, if you have Monopoly in your house, you can make it a rule that everyone must answer a prompt in order to buy a property. Or you can replace the "Chance" cards with prompt cards. Nearly any game available at home can become a therapy game if you add skill questions, discussion prompts, and so on. Playing these games can also help you spend more time with your loved ones and increase your knowledge and understanding of one another.

POSITIVE PSYCHOLOGY EXERCISES

The first positive psychology exercise is a Self-Care Vision Board. This can cultivate your self-care practices, self-compassion, creativity, inspiration, and motivation in a fun and playful way. Self-care is the active and conscious practice of activities that take good care of your own mental, emotional, and physical health. You must be able to attend to and meet your personal needs through self-care to take responsibility for yourself. Self-care is an effective way to increase your self-esteem (as your actions are telling you that you're worthy of being cared for) and increase your empathy (as your care for yourself can heighten your sense of connection with humanity). Taking care of yourself will also have obvious health benefits as your immune system will improve, your diet will be healthier, and you will generally have lower levels of anxiety and depression. Self-care can even improve your self-awareness, self-regulation, coping skills, and balancing of yourself and others. To do this exercise, follow these steps:

- Think of as many possible self-care activities as possible. Make sure that the ideas you come up with are relevant to you and are activities that you would actually enjoy completing and that fit with your values and lifestyle.
- For each activity that makes the cut, find some inspiring quotes and positive images that can relate to them and represent them. Brainstorm words and phrases that correspond to each self-care activity.

- Assemble your vision board and put it in a noticeable, visible, prominent place. This vision board will act as a visual representation of your ideas of self-care, reminding and motivating you to implement and improve your self-care.

The second exercise is The Guest House Poem. This exercise can help you accept yourself, improve your mindfulness, practice emotional intelligence, and explore your negative emotions. You will emphasize to yourself that emotions are fleeting and temporary and that even unpleasant and uncomfortable emotions have their value. This exercise can explain mindfulness to you and the importance of acknowledging and accepting difficult, unpleasant emotions. This will prevent you from suppressing your negative emotions, which is a habit that can lead to anxiety, depression, and poor mental health in general. When you try to control or ignore your uncomfortable emotions and thoughts, you tend to inadvertently give them more power over you, which can lead to more psychological problems. But by welcoming your negative emotions and thoughts as visitors to your house, the intensity and effect of those emotions can be diminished. For this exercise, you will read through the poem "The Guest House" by Jelaluddin Rumi. This poem describes being human as being a guest house where emotions are personified as temporary visitors that you should welcome even if they're not pleasant. This can help you imagine and remember that emotions aren't permanent residents in your house. They are temporary visitors who can be welcomed and invited to stay for a while before they eventually leave. Below is "The Guest House" by Jelaluddin Rumi (n.d.):

This being human is a guest house.
Every morning a new arrival.
A joy, a depression, a meanness,
some momentary awareness comes
as an unexpected visitor.
Welcome and entertain them all!
Even if they're a crowd of sorrows,
who violently sweep your house
empty of its furniture,
still, treat each guest honorably.
He may be clearing you out
for some new delight.
The dark thought, the shame, the malice,

meet them at the door laughing,
and invite them in.
Be grateful for whoever comes,
because each has been sent
as a guide from beyond.

After you read and reflect on this poem, ask yourself these questions:

- How do you interpret this poem?
- What emotions visit you most often? Why do you think that's the case?
- What would happen if you welcomed all your emotions rather than trying to ignore or deny them?
- What benefits could there be in welcoming your negative, unpleasant emotions?
- Can you relate to the line "violently sweeps your house empty of its furniture"? Have you ever felt this way?
- How can you apply the message of this poem to your everyday life?

The third positive psychology exercise is called Passengers on a Bus. This exercise can teach you what your values are, how to accept yourself, what emotions you're feeling, and how to overcome self-criticism. You will explore the ways in which your memories, thoughts, and emotions can drive your life. And this exploration will be done using metaphors, which are effective and meaningful ways for you to communicate about experiences and fill the experiential gap between what is and what can be. The Passengers on a Bus metaphor helps you describe how your internal experiences are driving your life and demonstrate the alternative possibility where those experiences don't control your life. Rather, they are accepted and welcomed to sit in the bus but not in the driver's seat. To do this exercise, imagine that you're a driver of a bus. The bus represents your mind, while the passengers on the bus represent your thoughts and emotions. As you drive along, some passengers sit calmly while others distract you by criticizing you or shouting directions. Within this metaphor, choose how you want to react to these passengers. This can help you realize that you can choose how to respond to those emotions and thoughts in real life. You can allow those passengers to shout and criticize while maintaining your focus on the road, the journey, and your goals.

Finally, some useful positive psychology tools are affirmations. These are positive phrases or statements that you can use to replace and challenge your negative thoughts. Simply have a few affirmations in mind that work for you and repeat them in the necessary and relevant circumstances. Of course, your negative thoughts and triggers will still occur, but these affirmations can lessen the physical and mental effects of those thoughts and triggers. This will then reduce your symptoms of anxiety. However, to benefit fully from positive affirmations, you must constantly practice. This will solidify the benefits you stand to gain from positive affirmations, such as improved integrity, efficacy, and self-identity. Positive affirmations can even increase certain neural pathways in your brain, improving certain cognitive functions that can benefit your mental health. For example, your ventromedial prefrontal cortex will become more active and efficient. This brain structure helps you analyze and deconstruct potentially harmful or threatening information. This will help you realize that certain things that scare you (such as social interactions) aren't actually threatening. Other than that, affirmations can decrease stress, improve performance (at school or work), decrease worry and fear, encourage positive lifestyle changes, and improve your physical behavior. You can repeat affirmations to yourself every day or even three to five times a day. This way, the message and sentiments of those affirmations will stay in your mind and be constantly reinforced to yourself. Additionally, you can simply repeat affirmations to yourself in your mind, set reminders on your phone, or write them on post-it notes around your house. Reading, saying, and repeating affirmations will be more effective than simply thinking them in your mind. When you take the time to say an affirmation out loud and repeat it, you will distract yourself from your negative thoughts, calm your mind, and enable yourself to change that negative thought. Affirmations are meant to be short, positive, encouraging, focused on the present, and focused on your strong points. Some general affirmations are:

- I am a successful person.
- I am confident in everything that I do.
- I am doing the best I can.
- I choose to be happy.
- I am in perfect health.

- I am resilient, so I will get through this difficult time.
- I believe in myself.
- I accept myself.
- I love myself.
- I don't judge myself.
- I don't compare myself to others.

Some affirmations meant to calm your anxiety are:

- I choose to feel calm.
- I choose positive and nurturing thoughts.
- I am right where I need to be.
- I do the best that I can.
- I forgive myself.
- I release the past.
- I look forward to a happy, bright future.
- I am safe.
- I inhale the good and exhale the bad.
- I am brave.
- I am strong.
- I will be okay.

You can even customize your affirmations to

specifically target some pain points for yourself. For example:

- I am not my anxiety.
- I am currently reducing my anxiety.
- I focus my energy on my values, not my anxiety.
- I have the strength to move beyond my anxiety.
- I am in charge of my breathing.
- I cultivate inner calm.
- I appreciate the beauty around me.
- I will survive.
- I have survived my anxiety before. I will survive now.
- I am curious about my triggers.
- I am patient.
- I take things one step at a time.
- I am present in this moment.
- I am not in danger; I am just uncomfortable.
- This too will pass.
- I do not deserve abuse.
- I am a good and kind person.
- I am talented and have many things to offer.

- I actively contribute to my healing.
- I enjoy making others laugh.
- I am an excellent listener.
- I have many supportive friends who help me.
- I liberate myself from this unhealthy relationship.
- I am a loyal friend and partner.
- I empathize with others.

BUILDING MENTAL TOUGHNESS

Mental toughness can help you get through your symptoms of social anxiety and improve your journey to better mental health. This trait refers to your ability to bounce back, to be strong yet flexible. If you have mental toughness, you will be able to adapt to changes, trauma, adversity, and threats. To cultivate mental toughness, you must practice positive thinking, visualization, goal setting, attention control, and anxiety control. These skills will help you develop the four main components of mental toughness which are control, commitment, challenge, and confidence. Control refers to how much you feel you're in control of your own life, such as your emotions and life purpose.

Commitment refers to your personal focus and reliability, so that this trait will help you effectively set and achieve your goals. Challenge refers to how driven and adaptable you are. You may see adversity and change as opportunities instead of threats so that you will be more agile and flexible. Confidence refers to how much you believe in your own ability to be capable and productive. And how much you believe you can influence others.

To develop mental toughness, one thing you can focus on is skill acquisition. By acquiring new skills, you can develop a sense of mastery and competence. These traits will help you face challenges, increase your self-esteem, and improve your problem-solving skills. You may try to improve your cognitive skills, such as memory or focus, or you may try out new hobbies to increase your competence in certain areas. The next thing to focus on to improve your mental toughness is goal setting. It's important to set goals that are achievable, actionable, feasible, and in line with your own values. These goals can be large or small and related to anything at all that you deem valuable in your life (such as religion, physical health, self-care, career, finance, and so on). Goals that intersect with skill acquisition will be doubly beneficial. For example, if your goal involves learning how to play a new instrument or learning a new language. Your goals will also be more beneficial if they work toward goals bigger than just yourself, for example, religious involvement or volunteering to help a specific cause. This can provide you with a sense of connection and purpose, which can then help you face challenges with more confidence. Moving on, you can focus on *controlled exposure*, where you gradually expose yourself to anxiety-inducing situations. This can help you overcome your fears. This activity can also intersect with skill acquisition. For example, if you fear public speaking, you can slowly expose yourself to this activity and acquire better public speaking skills in the process. Successful exposure will increase your self-esteem, sense of autonomy, pride, and sense of mastery. You can also try turning anxiety into progress. Your brain has plasticity, which means that it can change to become more or less resilient. If you keep feeding your anxiety, your brain will learn to become less resilient. But if you teach yourself to calm down, reassess your situation, reframe your thoughts, and make smarter decisions, your brain will learn to become more resilient. This doesn't mean that you have to completely change the distressing emotions that you usually feel. In fact, you can learn to accept those emotions, not judge them as negative or positive, and simply utilize them to your advantage. For example, anger can lower your focus and ability to perform, but it can also motivate you, sharpen your attention, and remind you of what's important to you. Fear can make you unwillingly remember your past failures, steal your attention, and lower your performance, but it can also make you more careful and considerate, deepen your thought process, and give you the chance to reassess your situation. Sadness can demotivate you and decrease your energy levels, but it can also push you to check your priorities and make changes to your environment and actions. Worry can make you procrastinate, but it can also make you improve your plans, adjust your expectations, and become more realistic. Frustration can decrease your motivation, but it can also challenge you to work harder and do better. Your emotions don't have to lead to negative effects. It all depends on how you choose to use them.

Going Out Into the World

You've now reached the end of this social anxiety CBT workbook for adults. Hopefully, by now you feel more prepared and motivated to address your social anxiety. All the information and practical exercises provided so far should make your journey much easier and more successful. Of course, facing your social anxiety and inner demons won't be a pleasant, simple, or comfortable task, but it is a worthwhile and necessary one. Social anxiety has stolen enough joy from your life. It's time you took a stand against it and made your own path in the world.

To help you remember all the information

provided, here is a short recap of each chapter. In Chapter 1, you studied social anxiety, what it is, and what it isn't. In Chapter 2, you learned about the accompanying demons that can provoke your social anxiety. In Chapter 3, you deepened your understanding of social anxiety by exploring its components, such as worry, fear, and panic. In Chapter 4, you understood CBT, how it works, and why it's a recommended method of therapy for social anxiety. In Chapter 5, you learned about cognitive distortions, how they affect you, and how you can use CBT exercises and positive psychology to overcome or challenge them. In Chapter 6, you were given more CBT exercises to help you challenge your self-conscious behavior, challenge your inner critic, and improve your social skills. In Chapter 7, you developed an understanding of mindfulness meditation, how it helps you, and how you can successfully practice it. In Chapter 8, you received some parting CBT games, positive psychology exercises, and tips on developing mental toughness that can help you deal with your everyday life.

The information in this book is aimed not only at helping you overcome your social anxiety, but also at improving your general quality of life and daily functioning. With all this information at your disposal, you can confidently go out into the world and forge your own happiness.

References

Araminta. (2021, November 5). *Social Anxiety Disorder and Its Link to Trauma*. Khiron Clinics. https://khironclinics.com/blog/social-anxiety-disorder-and-its-link-to-trauma/#:~:text=Studies%20have%20demonstrated%20a%20direct

Blurt Team. (2018, November 29). *Understanding The Difference Between Nervousnesss And Anxiety*. The Blurt Foundation. https://www.blurtitout.org/2018/11/29/difference-nervousness-anxiety/

Cherry, K. (2021). *Cognitive behavioral therapy*. Verywell Mind. https://www.verywellmind.com/what-is-cognitive-behavior-therapy-2795747

Cuncic, A. (2019). *The Surprising Similarities Between Shyness and Social Anxiety*. Verywell Mind. https://www.verywellmind.com/difference-between-shyness-and-social-anxiety-disorder-3024431

Gordon, J. P. (2019). *Low self-esteem and social anxiety*. Www.counselling-Directory.org.uk. https://www.counselling-directory.org.uk/memberarticles/low-self-esteem-and-social-anxiety

Mayo Clinic. (2018, May 4). *Panic attacks and panic disorder - Symptoms and causes*. Mayo Clinic. https://www.mayoclinic.org/diseases-conditions/panic-attacks/symptoms-causes/syc-20376021

Mayo Clinic. (2017, August 29). *Social anxiety disorder (social phobia) - symptoms and causes*. Mayo Clinic; Mayo Clinic. https://www.mayoclinic.org/diseases-conditions/social-anxiety-disorder/symptoms-causes/syc-20353561

NHS. (2021, February 16). *Panic disorder*. Nhs.uk. https://www.nhs.uk/mental-health/conditions/panic-disorder/

PsychCentral. (2022, August 17). *PTSD and Social Anxiety: The Connection.* Psych Central. https://psychcentral.com/ptsd/childhood-trauma-social-anxiety

Rumi, J. (n.d.). *The Guest House.* The Poetry Exchange. https://www.thepoetryexchange.co.uk/the-guest-house-by-rumi

South African Depression and Anxiety Group. (2004). *Fast facts about social phobia.* https://www.walshmedicalmedia.com/open-access/fast-facts-about-social-phobia-jop-7-052.pdf

Printed in Great Britain
by Amazon